About the Author

Almost thirty years in the trenches of financial technology hasn't dimmed my excitement for what's next. I'm still a curious technologist exploring the potential of AI to transform the financial services landscape. This book, born from my AI exploration, showcases one powerful use case: how AI can reshape everyday operations documentation. Come with me on this journey – let's discover the future of finance, one revolutionized process at a time.

My passion lies in crafting groundbreaking, reliable, and secure solutions. Years of experience in architectural design and system orchestration have honed my ability to translate complex theories into practical systems. I navigate the ever-evolving tech landscape with ease, enabling organizations to extract actionable insights and thrive in the digital age.

But even seasoned veterans like me recognize the need for clear, accessible knowledge. In this book, I combine my practical experience, with an AI-powered approach to curate and distill complex information into a readily digestible form. Think of me as your guide, using AI as a tool to navigate the often-murky waters of financial technology documentation.

This book isn't just for me – it's for all the new faces thrust into the world of Fintech, yearning for a crash course in navigating its intricacies. By sharing my journey, I hope to demystify AI's potential in generating documentation and equip you with the knowledge to embrace these transformative technologies with confidence.

Disclaimer

The information contained in this book is for informational purposes only and is not intended to be a substitute for professional advice. While all attempts have been made to verify the information provided, the author and publisher make no warranties, express or implied, with respect to its accuracy, completeness, or timeliness.

The authors and publisher shall not be liable for any damages arising out of the use of the information contained in this book. This includes, but is not limited to, damages for errors, omissions, or technical inaccuracies.
Readers are encouraged to seek professional guidance relevant to their specific circumstances before making any decisions or taking any actions based on the information contained in this book.

Table of Contents

INTRODUCTION

In the fast-paced and ever-evolving world of software, the role of the product manager has never been more critical. Software product managers are the visionaries, strategists, and orchestrators who bridge the gap between technology, business, and the end-user. They are the driving force behind the creation of innovative, user-friendly, and commercially successful software products.

This book is your comprehensive guide to the art and science of software product management. Whether you're an aspiring product manager, a seasoned professional, or a curious learner, this book will equip you with the knowledge, tools, and strategies needed to thrive in this dynamic field.

Within these pages, you'll discover:

- **The Fundamentals:** A deep dive into the core principles, responsibilities, and skills required for successful product management.
- **The Process:** A step-by-step journey through the entire product lifecycle, from ideation and discovery to launch and optimization.
- **The Strategies:** Proven techniques for defining a compelling product vision, conducting market research, prioritizing features, managing development teams, and launching products with impact.
- **The Trends:** Insights into the latest trends and technologies shaping the future of software product management, including AI, data-driven decision-making, and customer-centric development.

This book is not just a theoretical guide. It's a practical handbook filled with real-world examples, case studies, templates, and frameworks that you can immediately apply to your own work. You'll learn from the successes and failures of other product managers, gain insights into industry best practices, and discover the tools and technologies that can help you streamline your workflow and maximize your impact.

Whether you're working on a consumer app, an enterprise software platform, or a cutting-edge SaaS solution, this book will empower you to build winning software products that deliver value to your customers and drive your organization's growth.

Welcome to the exciting world of software product management! Let's embark on this journey together.

PART 1 Foundations of Software Product Management

Chapter 1: Evolution of the Role: From Visionary to Value Driver

In the ever-changing landscape of technology, the role of the software product manager has undergone a remarkable transformation. Once viewed primarily as a feature advocate or project coordinator, today's product managers are strategic leaders, customer champions, and data-driven decision-makers. They are the architects of product vision, the orchestrators of cross-functional teams, and the guardians of user experience.

This chapter will trace the evolution of the product management role, exploring its origins, key milestones, and the forces that have shaped its current form. We will delve into the diverse responsibilities and skills required of modern product managers, highlighting the importance of strategic thinking, market awareness, technical acumen, and leadership. By understanding the historical context and the ever-expanding scope of the role, you will gain a deeper appreciation for the unique challenges and opportunities that lie ahead for product managers in the digital age.

Whether you're a seasoned product manager seeking to refine your skills or an aspiring professional looking to enter the field, this chapter will provide a solid foundation for understanding the dynamic and multifaceted world of software product management.

1.1 What is Software Product Management?

At its core, software product management is the art and science of creating, launching, and continuously improving software products that deliver value to customers and drive business success. It is a multi-faceted discipline that encompasses a wide range of activities, from market research and strategic planning to product development, marketing, and customer success.

Product managers are the driving force behind the entire product lifecycle. They are responsible for:

- **Defining the product vision and strategy:** Product managers articulate a clear vision for the product, aligning it with the company's overall goals and objectives. They develop a comprehensive product strategy that outlines the target market, value proposition, and key differentiators.
- **Conducting market research and competitive analysis:** Product managers deeply understand the market landscape, customer needs, and competitive forces. They gather data and insights to inform product decisions and ensure the product meets market demands.
- **Prioritizing features and managing the product backlog:** Product managers prioritize features based on their potential impact on customer satisfaction, business goals, and technical feasibility. They maintain a well-organized product backlog that guides the development process.
- **Collaborating with cross-functional teams:** Product managers work closely with designers, engineers, marketers, sales representatives, and customer support teams to ensure the product is developed, launched, and supported effectively.

- **Launching and marketing the product:** Product managers create go-to-market strategies, develop marketing plans, and oversee the product launch. They ensure the product is positioned correctly in the market and reaches the right audience.
- **Measuring product success and iterating:** Product managers define key performance indicators (KPIs) and use data to track product performance. They analyze data, gather feedback, and use these insights to continuously improve the product.

In essence, software product managers are the CEOs of their products. They are responsible for the overall success of the product, from conception to retirement. They are the bridge between the business, technology, and the customer, ensuring that the product meets the needs of all stakeholders.

It's important to note that software product management is not a one-size-fits-all discipline. The specific responsibilities and activities of a product manager can vary depending on the company, product, and stage of the product lifecycle. However, the core principles of product management remain the same: to create products that customers love and that drive business success.

1.2 The Evolution of Software Product Management

The role of the software product manager has evolved significantly over the past few decades, mirroring the rapid advancements in technology and the changing landscape of the software industry. To truly understand the significance of the modern product manager, it's essential to trace the roots of the role and its transformation over time.

The Early Days: Brand Managers and Project Coordinators (1960s-1980s)

In the early days of software development, the concept of a dedicated product manager was not yet established. Instead, responsibilities for overseeing product development were often shared among different roles, such as brand managers or project coordinators.

- **Brand Managers:** These individuals were typically responsible for marketing and promoting products, but they often lacked the technical expertise to effectively guide the development process.
- **Project Coordinators:** These individuals focused on managing project timelines and resources, but they often lacked the strategic vision and customer focus needed to create successful products.

The Rise of the Product Manager (1990s-2000s)

As the software industry matured, the need for a dedicated role to oversee the entire product lifecycle became increasingly apparent. The rise of agile development methodologies, the increasing complexity of software products, and the growing emphasis on customer-centricity all contributed to the emergence of the software product manager as a distinct and essential role.

During this period, product managers began to take on a more strategic role, focusing on:

- **Market Research and Analysis:** Understanding customer needs, market trends, and competitive forces.

- **Product Strategy and Roadmapping:** Defining the product vision, setting strategic goals, and creating roadmaps to guide development.
- **Feature Prioritization and Backlog Management:** Deciding which features to build and when, based on customer value, business objectives, and technical feasibility.
- **Cross-Functional Collaboration:** Working closely with engineering, design, marketing, and sales teams to ensure alignment and effective execution.

The Modern Product Manager: Data-Driven Strategists and Customer Advocates (2010s-Present)

In the current digital age, the role of the product manager has continued to evolve, driven by factors such as the rise of big data, the increasing importance of user experience, and the growing demand for personalized products and services.

Today's product managers are expected to be:

- **Data-Driven Decision Makers:** They use data and analytics to inform every aspect of product development, from feature prioritization to go-to-market strategies.
- **Customer Champions:** They are deeply empathetic to customer needs and pain points, and they advocate for the user throughout the product lifecycle.
- **Agile Leaders:** They embrace agile development methodologies and foster a culture of experimentation and continuous improvement.
- **Technologically Savvy:** They have a solid understanding of the technologies that power their

products and the emerging trends that are shaping the industry.

The evolution of the software product manager is a testament to the dynamic nature of the software industry. As technology continues to advance at an unprecedented pace, the role of the product manager will undoubtedly continue to evolve, demanding new skills, new strategies, and a relentless focus on delivering value to customers.

1.3 The Role of the Product Manager (PM)

The product manager is the central figure in the software product development process, acting as a conductor orchestrating a symphony of diverse talents and perspectives. They are the glue that binds together the various stakeholders, ensuring that the product vision is clearly articulated, the development process is well-managed, and the final product delivers value to customers and drives business success.

The PM as the Voice of the Customer

One of the most critical responsibilities of a product manager is to be the voice of the customer. This means deeply understanding the needs, desires, and pain points of the target audience. Product managers conduct extensive market research, gather customer feedback, and use data analytics to gain insights into customer behavior and preferences. They use this information to inform every aspect of the product, from feature prioritization to user interface design.

The PM as the Product Strategist

Product managers are responsible for developing a comprehensive product strategy that aligns with the company's overall goals and objectives. This strategy outlines the target market, the product's value proposition, and the key differentiators that set it apart from the competition. The product strategy serves as a roadmap for the entire development process, guiding decisions about feature prioritization, resource allocation, and marketing initiatives.

The PM as the Product Owner

In the agile development framework, the product manager often takes on the role of the product owner. This means they are responsible for managing the product backlog, prioritizing features, and ensuring that the development team is working on the most impactful items. The product owner works closely with the development team, providing guidance and feedback to ensure that the product meets the defined requirements and delivers value to customers.

The PM as the Cross-Functional Collaborator

Product managers work closely with a wide range of stakeholders across the organization, including engineers, designers, marketers, sales representatives, and customer support teams. They facilitate communication and collaboration among these diverse groups, ensuring that everyone is aligned with the product vision and working towards a common goal. Product managers are skilled communicators, negotiators, and relationship builders, able to navigate complex organizational dynamics and foster a sense of shared purpose.

The PM as the Data-Driven Decision Maker

In today's data-rich environment, product managers are expected to be data-driven decision-makers. They use analytics tools and techniques to track product usage, measure key performance indicators (KPIs), and gather customer feedback. They analyze this data to identify trends, understand customer behavior, and make informed decisions about product improvements and new feature development. By leveraging data, product managers can ensure that the product is continuously evolving to meet the changing needs of the market and deliver maximum value to customers.

In conclusion, the role of the software product manager is multifaceted and demanding, requiring a unique blend of strategic thinking, technical acumen, interpersonal skills, and data-driven decision-making. It is a role that is constantly evolving, as technology advances and customer expectations change. However, the core responsibilities of the product manager remain the same: to be the voice of the customer, the product strategist, the product owner, the cross-functional collaborator, and the data-driven decision-maker.

1.4 Key Skills and Qualities of Successful PMs

The role of a software product manager demands a diverse skill set that blends strategic thinking, technical acumen, interpersonal prowess, and a deep understanding of the customer. While the specific requirements can vary depending on the industry, company size, and product complexity, several key skills and qualities are universally essential for success in this field.

Strategic Thinking and Vision:

Successful product managers are visionaries who can articulate a compelling product strategy that aligns with the company's overall goals. They possess the ability to think strategically, analyze market trends, identify opportunities, and develop roadmaps that guide the product's development and growth.

Customer Focus and Empathy:

A deep understanding of the customer is at the heart of effective product management. Product managers must be able to empathize with customer needs and pain points, translate those insights into product requirements, and champion the user throughout the development process. They constantly seek customer feedback, conduct user research, and prioritize features that deliver the most value to the end-user.

Data-Driven Decision-Making:

In the digital age, data is the lifeblood of product management. Successful PMs are adept at using data analytics to track product performance, measure key metrics, and make informed decisions about product improvements and new feature development. They leverage data to identify trends, understand user behavior, and validate assumptions, ensuring that the product is continuously evolving to meet market demands.

Communication and Collaboration:

Product managers act as a central hub of communication, collaborating with diverse stakeholders across the organization. They must be able to effectively communicate the product vision, articulate requirements, manage expectations, and resolve conflicts. Strong communication skills, both written and verbal, are essential for building consensus, fostering collaboration, and ensuring alignment among cross-functional teams.

Technical Acumen:

While product managers are not expected to be software engineers, a solid understanding of the technical aspects of the product is crucial. This knowledge allows them to communicate effectively with engineers, make informed decisions about technical trade-offs, and understand the feasibility and impact of different product features.

Leadership and Influence:

Product managers are leaders who inspire and motivate their teams. They possess the ability to influence without authority, build consensus, and rally support for the product vision. They foster a culture of collaboration, empower team members to take ownership, and celebrate successes along the way.

Problem-Solving and Adaptability:

The product development process is rarely smooth sailing. Unexpected challenges, shifting priorities, and changing market conditions are the norm. Successful product managers are agile problem solvers who can quickly adapt to changing circumstances, identify creative solutions, and keep the project on track.

Business Acumen:

A strong understanding of business principles and financial metrics is essential for product managers. They must be able to assess the market opportunity, develop pricing strategies, manage budgets, and measure the product's return on investment (ROI). They also need to understand the competitive landscape and be able to position the product effectively in the market.

By cultivating these key skills and qualities, product managers can effectively navigate the complex world of software product development, build winning products, and drive business success.

In addition to these core skills, successful product managers often possess a passion for technology, a strong work ethic, a curious and inquisitive mind, and a willingness to take risks and learn from failures. They are lifelong learners who are constantly seeking to expand their knowledge and skills, staying abreast of the latest trends and technologies in the ever-evolving field of software product management.

Chapter 2: Product Strategy and Vision: Charting the Course to Success

At the heart of every successful software product lies a clear and compelling vision, coupled with a well-defined strategy to bring that vision to life. The product vision serves as the North Star, guiding the team towards a shared goal and inspiring them to create something truly exceptional. The product strategy, on the other hand, is the roadmap that outlines the path to achieving that vision, detailing the steps, priorities, and resources needed to reach the destination.

In this chapter, we will delve into the critical components of product strategy and vision, exploring how they intersect, influence each other, and ultimately shape the success of a software product. We will examine the process of crafting a compelling vision that resonates with both internal stakeholders and target customers. We will also explore the intricacies of developing a robust product strategy that takes into account market dynamics, competitive landscape, resource constraints, and user needs.

You will learn how to:

- **Craft a compelling product vision statement:** A concise and inspiring declaration that encapsulates the essence of your product and its potential impact on the world.
- **Conduct thorough market research:** Gathering and analyzing data to gain insights into customer needs, market trends, and competitive forces.

- **Identify target customers and user personas:** Creating detailed profiles of your ideal users, understanding their motivations, pain points, and desired outcomes.
- **Define the product's value proposition:** Articulating the unique benefits that your product offers to customers and differentiating it from the competition.
- **Develop a comprehensive product strategy:** Creating a roadmap that outlines the steps, priorities, and resources needed to achieve the product vision.

By mastering the art of product strategy and vision, you will be well-equipped to lead your team on a successful journey, creating software products that not only meet market demands but also exceed customer expectations and drive sustainable growth. This chapter will provide you with the tools and frameworks needed to navigate the complexities of product strategy and vision, empowering you to create a clear and compelling direction for your product and your team.

2.1 Defining the Product Vision and Strategy

The product vision and strategy are the twin pillars upon which successful software products are built. They provide the direction, purpose, and roadmap for the entire product development journey. A clear and compelling vision inspires and motivates the team, while a well-defined strategy outlines the path to achieving that vision.

The Product Vision: A Beacon of Inspiration

The product vision is a concise and aspirational statement that articulates the long-term goal and desired impact of the product. It answers the fundamental questions of "why" and "what" – why does this product exist, and what does it aim to achieve in the world?

A powerful product vision:

- **Inspires and motivates:** It creates a sense of purpose and excitement among the team, aligning everyone around a shared goal.
- **Guides decision-making:** It serves as a filter for evaluating ideas and prioritizing features, ensuring that every decision aligns with the overarching vision.
- **Attracts customers and stakeholders:** It communicates the value and potential impact of the product, resonating with both internal and external audiences.

Examples of compelling product vision statements:

- **Tesla:** "To accelerate the world's transition to sustainable energy."
- **Airbnb:** "To create a world where anyone can belong anywhere."
- **Slack:** "To make work life simpler, more pleasant, and more productive."

Crafting a product vision:

1. **Start with the "why":** Clearly articulate the problem the product aims to solve or the need it fulfills.
2. **Envision the future:** Describe the ideal state that the product will help create for users and the world.
3. **Keep it concise and memorable:** Use clear, simple language that is easy to understand and remember.

4. **Make it aspirational and inspiring:** Capture the imagination and motivate the team to achieve the vision.

The Product Strategy: A Roadmap to Success

The product strategy is a comprehensive plan that outlines how the product vision will be achieved. It translates the high-level vision into actionable steps, defining the target market, value proposition, key differentiators, and go-to-market strategy.

A well-defined product strategy:

- **Provides a clear direction:** It helps the team focus their efforts on the most impactful activities.
- **Aligns the team:** It ensures that everyone understands the priorities and works towards a common goal.
- **Enables effective decision-making:** It provides a framework for evaluating trade-offs and making informed choices.
- **Measures progress:** It defines key metrics and milestones to track progress and success.

Components of a product strategy:

1. **Target market:** Clearly define the customer segments the product will serve.
2. **Value proposition:** Articulate the unique benefits the product offers to customers.
3. **Key differentiators:** Identify the factors that set the product apart from the competition.
4. **Go-to-market strategy:** Outline how the product will be launched, marketed, and sold.

5. **Roadmap:** Create a timeline of releases and milestones that guide the development process.

The Interplay Between Vision and Strategy

The product vision and strategy are interconnected and mutually reinforcing. The vision sets the direction, while the strategy provides the roadmap to get there. A strong vision inspires a robust strategy, and a well-crafted strategy helps to realize the vision.

By defining a clear and compelling product vision and developing a comprehensive product strategy, you set the stage for creating a successful software product that delivers value to customers, drives business growth, and makes a lasting impact in the world.

2.2 Conducting Market Research and Competitive Analysis

A successful product strategy is not built in a vacuum. It requires a deep understanding of the market landscape, customer needs, and competitive forces. This is where market research and competitive analysis come into play. These crucial activities provide the data and insights needed to make informed product decisions, identify opportunities, and mitigate risks.

Market Research: Understanding Your Customers

Market research is the systematic gathering and analysis of information about target markets and customers. It involves collecting data on customer demographics, preferences, behaviors, and pain points. This information can be gathered through various methods, including:

- **Surveys and questionnaires:** Gathering quantitative data on customer opinions, preferences, and behaviors.
- **Interviews and focus groups:** Conducting in-depth qualitative research to understand customer motivations, needs, and pain points.
- **Observational research:** Observing customers interacting with products or services to gain insights into their usage patterns and preferences.
- **Data analysis:** Analyzing existing data sources, such as industry reports, market trends, and social media conversations.

The goal of market research is to gain a comprehensive understanding of the target market and customer needs. This information can be used to:

- **Validate product ideas:** Ensure that the product concept resonates with potential customers and addresses their needs.
- **Identify target customer segments:** Define specific customer groups that the product will serve.
- **Develop user personas:** Create detailed profiles of ideal customers, their goals, motivations, and pain points.
- **Inform product design and development:** Tailor the product to meet the specific needs and preferences of the target audience.
- **Develop marketing and sales strategies:** Target the right customers with the right messaging and channels.

Competitive Analysis: Knowing Your Rivals

Competitive analysis involves evaluating the strengths, weaknesses, opportunities, and threats (SWOT) of competing products and companies. It helps product managers understand the competitive landscape, identify potential differentiators, and develop strategies to outperform rivals.

Competitive analysis typically involves:

- **Identifying key competitors:** Researching and identifying the main players in the market.
- **Analyzing competitor products:** Evaluating the features, pricing, marketing, and overall value proposition of competing products.
- **Assessing competitor strengths and weaknesses:** Identifying areas where competitors excel and areas where they fall short.
- **Understanding competitor strategies:** Analyzing how competitors are positioning themselves in the market and their go-to-market strategies.
- **Identifying opportunities and threats:** Recognizing potential market gaps or areas where the product can differentiate itself.

The insights gained from competitive analysis can be used to:

- **Differentiate the product:** Identify unique features or benefits that set the product apart from the competition.
- **Develop competitive strategies:** Create strategies to address competitive threats and capitalize on opportunities.
- **Inform product positioning:** Position the product in the market to highlight its unique strengths and appeal to the target audience.

By conducting thorough market research and competitive analysis, product managers can gain a deep understanding of the market landscape, customer needs, and competitive forces. This knowledge enables them to make informed decisions about product strategy, feature prioritization, marketing, and sales. The insights gained from these activities are essential for building successful products that meet market demands, deliver value to customers, and outperform the competition.

2.3 Identifying Target Customers and User Personas

Once you have a firm grasp of the market landscape and competitive forces, the next crucial step in defining your product strategy is to identify your target customers and develop user personas. This process involves narrowing down your focus from the broad market to specific customer segments that your product will serve, and then creating detailed representations of these ideal users.

Target Customers: Defining Your Niche

Your target customers are the specific groups of people or organizations that are most likely to benefit from your product and become paying customers. Identifying your target customers involves:

1. **Segmentation:** Divide the market into distinct groups based on shared characteristics, such as demographics, psychographics, behaviors, or needs.
2. **Targeting:** Evaluate each segment based on its size, growth potential, profitability, and alignment with your product's value proposition.
3. **Positioning:** Develop a clear and compelling message that resonates with your target customers

and differentiates your product from the competition.

By focusing on specific target customers, you can:

- **Tailor your product:** Develop features and functionalities that meet the specific needs and preferences of your target audience.
- **Optimize your marketing:** Craft targeted messaging and campaigns that appeal to your ideal customers.
- **Increase customer acquisition and retention:** Attract and retain customers who are more likely to be satisfied with your product and become loyal advocates.

User Personas: Bringing Your Customers to Life

User personas are fictional representations of your ideal customers, based on real data and insights gathered through market research. They are detailed profiles that include information about the user's:

- **Demographics:** Age, gender, location, occupation, income level, etc.
- **Psychographics:** Values, interests, lifestyle, personality, motivations, etc.
- **Behaviors:** How they use technology, their online habits, their purchasing behavior, etc.
- **Goals:** What they want to achieve with your product.
- **Pain points:** The challenges or frustrations they face that your product can solve.

User personas help product managers:

- **Empathize with customers:** Understand their needs, motivations, and pain points on a deeper level.
- **Make informed product decisions:** Prioritize features, design user interfaces, and develop marketing messages that resonate with target users.
- **Communicate effectively with stakeholders:** Share a common understanding of the target audience across the organization.
- **Test and validate product ideas:** Gather feedback from users who fit the persona profiles to ensure the product meets their needs.

Creating user personas:

1. **Gather data:** Conduct thorough market research, including surveys, interviews, focus groups, and data analysis.
2. **Identify patterns:** Look for commonalities and differences among your target customers.
3. **Develop personas:** Create detailed profiles that capture the essence of each customer segment.
4. **Validate and refine:** Test your personas with real users and refine them as needed.

By identifying your target customers and developing user personas, you can create a laser-focused product strategy that aligns with the needs and preferences of your ideal users. This will increase the likelihood of your product's success in the market and ensure that you are delivering value to the right people.

2.4 Defining the Value Proposition and Unique Selling Points

A compelling value proposition and clear unique selling points are essential for differentiating your product in a crowded market and attracting the right customers. These elements are at the core of your product strategy and marketing messaging, communicating the value your product brings to customers and what sets it apart from the competition.

The Value Proposition: Why Customers Should Choose You

A value proposition is a concise statement that articulates the specific benefits that your product offers to customers and why they should choose it over alternatives. It answers the fundamental question of "What's in it for me?" from the customer's perspective.

A strong value proposition:

- **Is customer-centric:** It focuses on the needs, desires, and pain points of the target audience.
- **Is clear and concise:** It communicates the benefits of the product in a simple and easy-to-understand manner.
- **Is specific and relevant:** It avoids generic claims and highlights the unique aspects of the product that matter most to customers.
- **Is credible and believable:** It is backed up by evidence, such as customer testimonials, data, or case studies.
- **Is differentiated:** It clearly articulates what sets the product apart from the competition.

Examples of strong value propositions:

- **Stripe:** "We make it easy to accept payments and run an internet business."
- **Shopify:** "The platform commerce is built on."
- **Zoom:** "Frictionless video meetings for teams and classrooms."

Developing a value proposition:

1. **Identify customer pain points:** Understand the challenges or frustrations that your target customers face.
2. **Map product benefits to pain points:** Clearly articulate how your product solves those problems or improves the customer's life.
3. **Highlight key differentiators:** Emphasize the unique aspects of your product that set it apart from the competition.
4. **Craft a concise and compelling statement:** Summarize the value proposition in a few sentences that are easy to understand and remember.
5. **Test and refine:** Get feedback from potential customers to ensure that the value proposition resonates with them.

Unique Selling Points (USPs): What Sets You Apart

Unique selling points are the specific features or benefits that differentiate your product from competitors. They are the reasons why customers should choose your product over others in the market.

Strong USPs:

- **Are meaningful to customers:** They address a significant pain point or provide a unique benefit that customers value.
- **Are defensible:** They are difficult for competitors to replicate.
- **Are communicable:** They can be easily explained and understood by customers.

Examples of unique selling points:

- **Apple:** "Intuitive design, seamless integration, and premium user experience."
- **Amazon:** "Vast selection, competitive prices, and fast and reliable delivery."
- **Salesforce:** "Customizable CRM platform with robust analytics and AI capabilities."

Identifying USPs:

1. **Analyze the competition:** Identify the strengths and weaknesses of competing products.
2. **Evaluate your product:** Assess the unique features, benefits, or technologies that your product offers.
3. **Gather customer feedback:** Ask customers what they value most about your product and what sets it apart from others.
4. **Prioritize and communicate:** Focus on the most impactful USPs and highlight them in your marketing and sales efforts.

A strong value proposition and clear USPs are essential for attracting and retaining customers. They help to establish your brand identity, differentiate your product, and build a loyal customer base. By clearly articulating the value you bring to customers and what sets you apart, you can create a competitive advantage that drives long-term success.

Product Strategy and Vision Action List

1. **Craft a Compelling Product Vision:**
   - Start with the "why": Identify the core problem or need your product addresses.
   - Envision the future: Describe the ideal state your product will create for users.
   - Keep it concise and memorable: Use clear, inspiring language that resonates.
2. **Develop a Robust Product Strategy:**
   - Define your target market: Identify specific customer segments you'll serve.
   - Articulate your value proposition: Clearly state the unique benefits your product offers.
   - Identify key differentiators: Determine what sets your product apart from the competition.
   - Outline your go-to-market strategy: Plan your product launch, marketing, and sales approach.
   - Create a roadmap: Develop a timeline of releases and milestones to guide development.
3. **Conduct Thorough Market Research:**
   - Gather data: Use surveys, interviews, focus groups, and data analysis to understand customer needs and preferences.
   - Validate product ideas: Ensure your concept resonates with potential customers and addresses their pain points.
4. **Perform a Competitive Analysis:**
   - Identify key competitors: Research the major players in your market.

- o Analyze competitor products: Evaluate their features, pricing, marketing, and overall value proposition.
- o Assess competitor strengths and weaknesses: Pinpoint areas where you can outshine them.

5. **Identify Target Customers and Create User Personas:**
    - o Segment the market: Divide the market into distinct groups based on shared characteristics.
    - o Target specific segments: Focus on the groups that are most likely to benefit from your product.
    - o Develop user personas: Create detailed profiles of your ideal customers, including their demographics, psychographics, behaviors, goals, and pain points.

By taking these actions, you will lay the foundation for a successful product strategy, ensuring your product is aligned with customer needs, market demands, and your company's overall goals. This strategic approach will increase your chances of creating a product that stands out in the market, attracts loyal customers, and ultimately drives business growth.

Chapter 3: Product Discovery and Planning: From Idea to Actionable Roadmap

The journey from a spark of an idea to a tangible, successful product is a complex and often unpredictable one. It requires a systematic approach to discovery and planning, a process where ideas are validated, features are prioritized, and a clear roadmap is charted. This chapter delves into the critical phase of product discovery and planning, where the foundation for a successful product launch is laid.

Product discovery is the exploratory phase where you gain a deep understanding of your customers' needs, pain points, and desires. It's about identifying problems worth solving and uncovering opportunities for innovation. This phase involves gathering feedback from potential users, analyzing market trends, and conducting experiments to validate assumptions.

Product planning, on the other hand, is the strategic phase where you translate your insights into a concrete plan of action. It involves defining the product scope, prioritizing features, estimating timelines, and creating a roadmap that guides the development process. This phase requires careful consideration of resources, technical feasibility, and business goals.

In this chapter, you will learn how to:

- **Generate and validate product ideas:** Tap into various sources of inspiration, gather feedback from potential users, and conduct experiments to test the viability of your ideas.

- **Define the product roadmap:** Create a visual representation of the product's evolution, outlining key milestones, features, and timelines.
- **Prioritize features and create a backlog:** Employ various prioritization frameworks to determine which features to build first, based on their impact on customer value and business goals.
- **Estimate and plan releases:** Break down the product development process into manageable chunks, estimate timelines, and allocate resources effectively.

By mastering the art of product discovery and planning, you will be equipped to make informed decisions about what to build, when to build it, and how to build it. This chapter will provide you with the tools, techniques, and frameworks to navigate the complexities of this critical phase, ensuring that your product development efforts are aligned with customer needs, market demands, and business objectives.

3.1 Idea Generation and Validation: Nurturing the Seeds of Innovation

The genesis of any successful software product begins with an idea—a spark of inspiration that has the potential to transform how people live, work, or interact with technology. However, not all ideas are created equal. Some may be brilliant but impractical, while others may be feasible but lack the market appeal necessary for success. The process of idea generation and validation is designed to filter out the noise and identify the ideas that are worth pursuing.

Idea Generation: Tapping into the Wellspring of Creativity

Generating new product ideas is a creative process that can be fueled by various sources:

- **Customer feedback and pain points:** Listen to your customers. Their feedback, suggestions, and complaints can be a goldmine of ideas for new features, improvements, or entirely new products.
- **Market trends and emerging technologies:** Stay abreast of the latest trends in your industry and explore how emerging technologies can be leveraged to create innovative solutions.
- **Internal brainstorming sessions:** Gather your team for brainstorming sessions, where ideas can be freely shared, discussed, and built upon.
- **Competitive analysis:** Analyze your competitors' products and services to identify gaps in the market or areas where you can offer a better solution.
- **User research and observation:** Observe how users interact with existing products and services to identify pain points, unmet needs, or opportunities for improvement.

Remember, the goal of idea generation is not to come up with the perfect idea right away, but to generate a wide range of possibilities that can be explored and refined.

Idea Validation: Separating the Wheat from the Chaff

Once you have a pool of potential product ideas, the next step is to validate them. This involves testing your assumptions about the problem, the solution, and the target market. Idea validation is a critical step that helps you avoid wasting time and resources on ideas that are not viable.

There are several methods for validating product ideas:

- **Customer interviews and surveys:** Talk to potential customers to get their feedback on your ideas. Ask them about their pain points, needs, and willingness to pay for a solution.
- **Prototyping and user testing:** Create a basic version of your product (a prototype) and test it with potential users. Observe how they interact with the prototype and gather feedback on its usability and value.
- **Market research and analysis:** Analyze market trends, competitor offerings, and industry reports to assess the potential demand for your product.
- **Minimum Viable Product (MVP):** Develop a bare-bones version of your product with just enough features to satisfy early adopters and gather feedback for further development.

The goal of idea validation is to gather enough evidence to determine whether an idea is worth pursuing. If an idea fails to gain traction during the validation process, it's better to pivot or abandon it early on, rather than investing significant time and resources in a product that may not succeed.

By following a structured approach to idea generation and validation, you can increase the likelihood of identifying winning product ideas that have the potential to resonate with customers, solve real problems, and drive business growth.

3.2 Defining the Product Roadmap: Your Strategic Path to Success

A product roadmap is a high-level visual representation of a product's intended evolution over time. It is a strategic document that outlines the direction, priorities, and progress of a product, providing a clear path to achieving the product vision.

A well-crafted roadmap serves as a shared source of truth for the entire team, aligning everyone around a common understanding of what will be built, when it will be built, and why. It is a dynamic document that evolves as the product and market landscape change, but it remains a valuable tool for guiding decision-making and ensuring that the product stays on track.

Key Components of a Product Roadmap:

- **Timeline:** The roadmap should have a clear timeline that indicates when specific features or milestones are expected to be completed. This can be represented in various ways, such as quarters, months, or specific dates, depending on the level of detail needed.
- **Themes:** Themes are high-level groupings of features or initiatives that align with the product strategy and vision. They provide a broader context for individual features and help to communicate the overall direction of the product.
- **Features and Initiatives:** These are the specific product enhancements or projects that will be undertaken to achieve the product vision. Each feature should have a clear description, estimated effort, and potential impact on customers and the business.

- **Status Indicators:** Visual indicators, such as color coding or progress bars, can be used to communicate the status of each feature or initiative. This helps stakeholders quickly understand what is in progress, what is planned, and what has been completed.
- **Release Markers:** These indicate planned releases or major milestones in the product's development lifecycle. They can help to manage expectations and coordinate efforts across different teams.

Types of Product Roadmaps:

There are various types of product roadmaps, each serving a different purpose and audience:

- **Strategy Roadmap:** This high-level roadmap focuses on communicating the long-term vision and strategic goals of the product. It is often used to align stakeholders and secure buy-in for the product direction.
- **Feature Roadmap:** This roadmap details the specific features or functionalities that will be developed over time. It is often used by product teams to prioritize work and manage the development backlog.
- **Release Roadmap:** This roadmap outlines the timeline and content of planned releases. It is used to communicate release dates to customers and stakeholders and to coordinate marketing and sales efforts.
- **Portfolio Roadmap:** This roadmap provides an overview of multiple products or projects within a portfolio. It is used to manage dependencies, allocate resources, and communicate the overall strategy across different product lines.

Best Practices for Creating a Product Roadmap:

- **Start with the Why:** Clearly articulate the product vision and strategic goals that the roadmap will support.
- **Involve Stakeholders:** Gather input from key stakeholders, including customers, executives, sales, marketing, and development teams.
- **Focus on Outcomes, Not Outputs:** Prioritize features based on their potential impact on customer value and business goals, rather than simply listing a laundry list of features.
- **Keep it High-Level:** Avoid getting bogged down in too much detail. The roadmap should provide a clear overview of the product's direction, not a detailed specification.
- **Be Flexible:** The roadmap is not set in stone. It should be a living document that evolves as the product and market landscape change.

By following these best practices, you can create a product roadmap that is both strategic and actionable, guiding your team towards success while remaining adaptable to change.

3.3 Prioritizing Features and Creating a Backlog: Building the Right Things, at the Right Time

With a clear product vision and roadmap in place, the next critical step is to determine which features to build and when. This is where feature prioritization and backlog management come into play. These processes ensure that your team focuses its efforts on the most impactful features that align with your product strategy and deliver maximum value to customers.

Feature Prioritization: A Balancing Act

Prioritizing features is not a simple task. It involves balancing a multitude of factors, including:

- **Customer Value:** How much value does the feature deliver to the customer? Does it solve a significant pain point or fulfill a critical need?
- **Business Value:** How does the feature contribute to the company's strategic goals? Does it increase revenue, reduce costs, or improve customer retention?
- **Effort and Cost:** How much time and resources will it take to develop and implement the feature?
- **Technical Feasibility:** Is the feature technically feasible to build with the available resources and technology?
- **Market Trends:** Is the feature aligned with current market trends and demands?
- **Competitive Landscape:** How does the feature compare to similar offerings from competitors?

There are numerous prioritization frameworks and techniques available to help product managers make these difficult decisions. Some popular methods include:

- **MoSCoW Method:** Categorizes features as Must-Have, Should-Have, Could-Have, and Won't-Have.
- **Value vs. Effort Matrix:** Plots features on a matrix based on their estimated value and effort, helping to identify high-value, low-effort opportunities.
- **RICE Scoring:** Quantifies the impact, reach, confidence, and effort of each feature to calculate a priority score.
- **Kano Model:** Categorizes features based on their potential to satisfy or delight customers.

The best prioritization method for your team will depend on your specific context, resources, and goals. It's important to experiment with different approaches and find the one that works best for you.

Creating the Product Backlog: Your Organized To-Do List

The product backlog is a dynamic list of all the features, enhancements, and bug fixes that are planned for the product. It is an essential tool for managing the development process, ensuring that the team is working on the right things at the right time.

The backlog is typically organized into a prioritized list, with the highest priority items at the top. This allows the team to focus on the most impactful features first and adapt to changing priorities as needed.

Key components of a product backlog:

- **User Stories:** Concise descriptions of features or functionalities from the user's perspective.
- **Acceptance Criteria:** Specific criteria that must be met for a user story to be considered complete.
- **Estimates:** Rough estimates of the effort required to complete each user story.
- **Priority:** A ranking that indicates the relative importance of each user story.

The backlog is a living document that is constantly being updated and refined. As new ideas emerge, feedback is gathered, and priorities shift, the backlog must be adjusted to reflect the latest information.

Best Practices for Backlog Management:

- **Regularly Groom the Backlog:** Review and update the backlog regularly to ensure that it reflects the current priorities and understanding of the product.
- **Break Down Large Items:** Decompose large user stories into smaller, more manageable tasks.
- **Refine Estimates:** Continuously refine estimates as more information becomes available.
- **Collaborate with Stakeholders:** Involve stakeholders in the backlog refinement process to ensure that their needs and priorities are considered.

By mastering the art of feature prioritization and backlog management, you can ensure that your team is building the right things at the right time, delivering maximum value to customers and driving the success of your product.

3.4 Estimating and Planning Releases: Navigating the Development Timeline

Estimating and planning releases is a crucial aspect of product management. It involves breaking down the development process into manageable chunks, forecasting timelines, and allocating resources effectively. This allows product managers to set realistic expectations, manage stakeholder communication, and ensure the timely delivery of valuable features to customers.

Estimation Techniques: Predicting the Unpredictable

Estimating the effort and time required to develop software features is inherently challenging. There are many variables involved, including the complexity of the feature, the team's experience and skills, the available resources, and unexpected obstacles that may arise along the way.

However, there are several estimation techniques that can help product managers make more informed forecasts:

- **Story Points:** This relative estimation technique involves assigning a numerical value (story points) to each user story based on its relative size and complexity compared to other stories. Story points are often used in Agile development to track team velocity and forecast future work.
- **T-Shirt Sizes:** This simple estimation method involves categorizing features as Small, Medium, Large, or Extra Large based on their perceived size and complexity. It is a quick and easy way to get a rough estimate, but it lacks the precision of more detailed methods.
- **Planning Poker:** This collaborative estimation technique involves team members anonymously estimating the effort required for each user story using a deck of cards with numerical values. The team then discusses the estimates and reaches a consensus.
- **Expert Judgment:** This involves seeking estimates from experienced team members or subject matter experts who have a deep understanding of the work involved.

It's important to note that no estimation technique is perfect. The best approach is often to use a combination of methods and to continuously refine estimates as more information becomes available.

Planning Releases: Creating a Roadmap to Delivery

Once you have estimated the effort required for each feature, you can start planning your releases. A release is a collection of features that are delivered to customers at a specific point in time. Release planning involves:

- **Defining Release Goals:** What are the key objectives of each release? What customer problems are you trying to solve?
- **Prioritizing Features:** Based on your estimates and release goals, prioritize the features that will be included in each release.
- **Creating a Release Schedule:** Develop a timeline for each release, including start and end dates, key milestones, and dependencies.
- **Allocating Resources:** Assign team members, budget, and other resources to each release to ensure that it can be delivered on time and within budget.
- **Managing Risks:** Identify potential risks that could impact the release schedule and develop mitigation plans.
- **Communicating with Stakeholders:** Keep stakeholders informed of release progress, changes in plans, and any potential risks.

Release planning is an iterative process. As you learn more about the project, you may need to adjust your release schedule, priorities, and resources. It's important to remain flexible and adaptable to ensure that your releases deliver value to customers and meet the needs of the business.

Key Considerations for Release Planning:

- **Balance Scope, Time, and Cost:** These three constraints are interrelated. Changing one will likely impact the others. Be realistic about what can be achieved within the available time and resources.

- **Prioritize Value Delivery:** Focus on delivering the most valuable features to customers as early as possible.
- **Communicate Early and Often:** Keep stakeholders informed of progress and any changes to the plan.
- **Be Agile:** Embrace change and be prepared to adjust your plan as needed.
- **Celebrate Successes:** Recognize and celebrate the team's achievements along the way.

By effectively estimating and planning your releases, you can ensure that your product development efforts are focused, efficient, and deliver value to customers in a timely manner. This is essential for building a successful product that meets market demands and drives business growth.

Product Discovery and Planning Action List

1. **Idea Generation:**
   - Gather customer feedback: Actively seek input from users through surveys, interviews, and feedback channels.
   - Analyze market trends: Stay up-to-date on industry developments and emerging technologies.
   - Conduct brainstorming sessions: Encourage your team to freely share and build upon ideas.
   - Perform competitive analysis: Identify gaps in the market or areas where you can offer a better solution.
   - Observe user behavior: Watch how users interact with your product and similar

products to uncover pain points and unmet needs.

2. **Idea Validation:**
   o Interview potential customers: Get direct feedback on your ideas and their willingness to pay for a solution.
   o Create prototypes: Build basic versions of your product to test with potential users.
   o Conduct user testing: Observe how users interact with your prototype and gather feedback.
   o Research the market: Analyze market trends and competitor offerings to assess demand for your product.
   o Build a Minimum Viable Product (MVP): Develop a basic version with essential features to gather early feedback.

3. **Define the Product Roadmap:**
   o Articulate your product vision: Clearly state the long-term goal and desired impact of your product.
   o Set strategic goals: Outline the key objectives that your product aims to achieve.
   o Prioritize themes and features: Determine which areas to focus on and which features to develop first.
   o Establish a timeline: Set milestones and deadlines for major releases and feature deliveries.
   o Communicate the roadmap: Share the roadmap with stakeholders to ensure alignment and manage expectations.

4. **Prioritize Features and Create a Backlog:**
   o Choose a prioritization framework: Select a method that best suits your team and product (e.g., MoSCoW, RICE, Kano Model).

- Gather input from stakeholders: Include customer feedback, business goals, and technical feasibility in your decision-making.
- Create a prioritized backlog: List all features, enhancements, and bug fixes in order of priority.
- Refine and update the backlog regularly: Adapt to new information and changing priorities.

5. **Estimate and Plan Releases:**
   - Choose an estimation technique: Select a method that works for your team and project (e.g., story points, planning poker).
   - Estimate effort for each feature: Determine the time and resources needed to develop each item in the backlog.
   - Define release goals: Set clear objectives for each release.
   - Create a release schedule: Plan the timing and content of each release.
   - Allocate resources: Assign team members, budget, and other resources to each release.
   - Manage risks: Identify and mitigate potential risks that could impact the release schedule.

By following this action list, you can create a structured and systematic approach to product discovery and planning. This will help you ensure that your product development efforts are focused, efficient, and deliver maximum value to your customers.

Part II: Building and Launching Software Products

Chapter 4: Product Design and Development: Transforming Vision into Reality

The transition from a conceptualized product to a tangible, functional software application is a thrilling yet intricate journey. This phase, encompassing product design and development, is where the carefully crafted vision and strategy of a product begin to materialize. It's a collaborative endeavor that brings together diverse talents—designers, engineers, product managers, and quality assurance specialists—all working in unison to breathe life into the product concept.

This chapter will delve into the multifaceted world of product design and development, exploring the processes, methodologies, and tools that drive the creation of successful software products. We will examine the critical role of user experience (UX) and user interface (UI) design in shaping user satisfaction and engagement. We will also delve into the intricacies of agile development methodologies, emphasizing the importance of iterative development, continuous feedback, and adaptability in the face of evolving requirements.

In this chapter, you will:

- **Understand the principles of user-centered design:** Learn how to create intuitive and engaging user interfaces that meet the needs and expectations of your target audience.

- **Explore the agile development process:** Gain insights into the iterative and collaborative approach that enables faster delivery of value and continuous improvement.
- **Learn to manage the development process effectively:** Discover strategies for prioritizing features, tracking progress, and ensuring quality throughout the development lifecycle.
- **Master the art of collaboration:** Understand how to foster effective communication and collaboration between designers, engineers, product managers, and other stakeholders.

By mastering the concepts and techniques presented in this chapter, you will be well-equipped to navigate the complexities of product design and development, ensuring that your product not only meets but exceeds user expectations, delivers on its value proposition, and achieves lasting success in the market.

4.1 Working with UX/UI Designers and Developers: A Symphony of Collaboration

The creation of a successful software product is not a solo endeavor. It requires the harmonious collaboration of diverse talents, each bringing their unique expertise to the table. In this section, we will focus on the crucial partnership between product managers, UX/UI designers, and developers, exploring how their collaboration shapes the user experience, functionality, and overall success of the product.

The Product Manager's Role: The Visionary and the Bridge

The product manager acts as the visionary leader, articulating the product vision and strategy. They translate market research, customer feedback, and business goals into clear product requirements. The PM serves as a bridge between the design and development teams, ensuring that the product's functionality aligns with the desired user experience.

Key responsibilities of the product manager in this collaboration:

- **Defining Product Requirements:** Clearly articulating the functional and non-functional requirements of the product, including features, user flows, and performance expectations.
- **Prioritizing Features:** Working with stakeholders to prioritize features based on their impact on user value and business goals.
- **Communicating the Vision:** Ensuring that designers and developers understand the product vision and goals, so they can make informed decisions throughout the development process.
- **Providing Feedback:** Reviewing design mockups and prototypes, providing constructive feedback to ensure that they meet the product requirements and user needs.
- **Managing Expectations:** Setting realistic expectations for timelines, resources, and scope, and communicating any changes or challenges to the team.

The UX/UI Designer's Role: The User Advocate and the Architect

UX/UI designers are the champions of user experience. They are responsible for creating intuitive, engaging, and aesthetically pleasing user interfaces that meet the needs and expectations of the target audience. They conduct user research, create wireframes and prototypes, and test their designs with real users to ensure usability and effectiveness.

Key responsibilities of the UX/UI designer in this collaboration:

- **Conducting User Research:** Gathering insights into user behaviors, preferences, and pain points through interviews, surveys, and usability testing.
- **Creating Wireframes and Prototypes:** Developing visual representations of the user interface, including the layout, navigation, and interactions.
- **Iterating on Designs:** Refining the designs based on feedback from the product manager, developers, and users.
- **Ensuring Usability and Accessibility:** Designing interfaces that are easy to use and accessible to users with disabilities.
- **Advocating for the User:** Championing user needs and ensuring that the final product delivers a positive and satisfying user experience.

The Developer's Role: The Builder and the Problem Solver

Developers are the builders of the product. They translate the design concepts into functional code, ensuring that the product performs as intended and meets the technical requirements. They are also responsible for optimizing performance, ensuring security, and fixing bugs.

Key responsibilities of the developer in this collaboration:

- **Technical Implementation:** Translating design mockups and prototypes into working code.
- **Problem-Solving:** Identifying and resolving technical challenges that arise during the development process.
- **Performance Optimization:** Ensuring that the product is fast, responsive, and scalable.
- **Security:** Implementing security measures to protect user data and prevent unauthorized access.
- **Bug Fixing:** Identifying and fixing bugs that are reported by users or discovered during testing.

The Importance of Collaboration:

The collaboration between product managers, UX/UI designers, and developers is essential for creating successful software products. By working together, these teams can:

- **Ensure alignment:** Ensure that everyone is working towards the same goals and that the product meets the needs of both users and the business.
- **Foster innovation:** Encourage creativity and generate new ideas by bringing together diverse perspectives.
- **Improve efficiency:** Streamline the development process by identifying and resolving issues early on.
- **Deliver high-quality products:** Create products that are both functional and user-friendly.

Effective collaboration requires open communication, mutual respect, and a willingness to compromise. By fostering a collaborative culture, product teams can unlock their full potential and create exceptional software products that delight users and drive business success.

4.2 Agile Development Methodologies: Embracing Flexibility and Collaboration

In the fast-paced world of software development, traditional, linear approaches like the Waterfall model often fall short in meeting the demands of rapidly changing requirements and evolving customer needs. Enter Agile development methodologies, a set of iterative and incremental approaches that prioritize flexibility, collaboration, and continuous delivery of value.

What is Agile Development?

Agile development is a philosophy and a set of values and principles outlined in the Agile Manifesto. It emphasizes:

- **Individuals and interactions:** Valuing people over processes and tools.
- **Working software:** Prioritizing the delivery of functional software over comprehensive documentation.
- **Customer collaboration:** Working closely with customers throughout the development process to ensure their needs are met.
- **Responding to change:** Embracing change rather than rigidly adhering to a plan.

Agile vs. Waterfall:

Feature	Agile Development	Waterfall Development
Planning	Iterative, adaptive planning	Detailed upfront planning
Development	Incremental, frequent releases	Sequential phases
Testing	Continuous testing throughout	Testing at the end of development
Customer Involvement	High, continuous collaboration	Limited to requirements gathering
Flexibility	High, embraces change	Low, resistant to change

Benefits of Agile Development:

- **Faster time to market:** Agile teams deliver working software in shorter iterations, allowing for faster feedback and course correction.
- **Increased customer satisfaction:** Regular customer collaboration ensures that the product meets their evolving needs.
- **Improved quality:** Continuous testing throughout the development process helps to identify and fix defects early on.
- **Enhanced team morale:** Agile teams are empowered to self-organize and make decisions, leading to increased motivation and engagement.
- **Reduced risk:** The iterative nature of agile development allows for early identification and mitigation of risks.

Common Agile Frameworks:

- **Scrum:** A popular agile framework that emphasizes self-organizing teams, time-boxed sprints, and daily stand-up meetings.
- **Kanban:** A visual workflow management method that focuses on limiting work in progress and optimizing flow.
- **Extreme Programming (XP):** An agile framework that emphasizes technical practices such as test-driven development, pair programming, and continuous integration.

Implementing Agile in Product Design and Development:

1. **Cross-functional Teams:** Create teams that include representatives from design, development, testing, and other relevant disciplines.
2. **User Stories:** Break down product features into smaller, manageable user stories that describe the desired functionality from the user's perspective.
3. **Iterations and Sprints:** Divide the development process into short, time-boxed iterations or sprints, typically lasting 1-4 weeks.
4. **Daily Stand-ups:** Hold daily meetings to discuss progress, identify blockers, and plan the day's work.
5. **Sprint Reviews:** Conduct regular reviews to demonstrate the completed work and gather feedback.
6. **Retrospectives:** Reflect on the sprint, identify areas for improvement, and plan for the next sprint.

Agile is a Mindset, Not Just a Methodology:

Agile development is not just a set of practices but a mindset that embraces collaboration, adaptability, and continuous improvement. It requires a shift in thinking from traditional command-and-control approaches to a more empowering and collaborative environment.

By adopting agile principles and practices, product teams can unlock their full potential, deliver high-quality software products faster, and adapt to the ever-changing demands of the market.

1. thetrendycoder.com/agile-cheat-sheet-for-beginners/

4.3 Managing the Development Process: Steering the Ship to Success

The software development process is a complex undertaking that involves multiple phases, diverse teams, and numerous dependencies. Effective management of this process is crucial to ensure that the product is delivered on time, within budget, and meets the desired quality standards. The product manager plays a pivotal role in steering the development ship, coordinating efforts, resolving issues, and keeping the project on track.

Key Responsibilities of the Product Manager in Development:

1. **Project Planning:** Collaborating with stakeholders to define the project scope, create a detailed project plan, and establish timelines and milestones.
2. **Resource Allocation:** Ensuring that the right resources—people, technology, and budget—are available at the right time to support the development process.

3. **Risk Management:** Identifying potential risks that could derail the project and developing mitigation plans to address them.
4. **Communication and Collaboration:** Facilitating communication and collaboration between different teams, ensuring that everyone is aligned with the project goals and working towards a common vision.
5. **Progress Tracking:** Monitoring the progress of the development team, tracking key metrics, and identifying any issues or roadblocks that may arise.
6. **Issue Resolution:** Working with the team to resolve technical, logistical, or interpersonal challenges that may impede progress.
7. **Quality Assurance:** Ensuring that the product meets the desired quality standards through regular testing and review.
8. **Release Management:** Coordinating the release of new features or updates, ensuring that they are thoroughly tested and ready for deployment.

Tools and Techniques for Managing the Development Process:

Product managers have a variety of tools and techniques at their disposal to help them manage the development process effectively. These include:

- **Project Management Software:** Tools like Jira, Asana, or Trello can help product managers create and manage project plans, track tasks, and monitor progress.
- **Agile Development Methodologies:** As discussed earlier, Agile methodologies provide a framework for iterative development, allowing for flexibility and continuous improvement.

- **Communication Tools:** Tools like Slack, Microsoft Teams, or Zoom facilitate communication and collaboration between team members, regardless of their location.
- **Data Analytics:** Product managers can use data analytics to track key metrics, identify bottlenecks, and make data-driven decisions to improve the development process.

Best Practices for Managing the Development Process:

- **Set Clear Goals and Expectations:** Clearly define the project goals, scope, and timelines at the outset. This will help to ensure that everyone is on the same page and working towards a common vision.
- **Prioritize Ruthlessly:** Not all features are created equal. Prioritize the features that deliver the most value to customers and align with the product strategy.
- **Communicate Early and Often:** Keep stakeholders informed of progress, challenges, and any changes to the plan. Transparent communication helps to build trust and manage expectations.
- **Empower the Team:** Give your team the autonomy to make decisions and solve problems. Trust their expertise and encourage them to take ownership of their work.
- **Celebrate Successes:** Recognize and reward the team for their hard work and achievements. This will help to boost morale and keep the team motivated.

By employing effective management practices, product managers can ensure that the development process runs smoothly, the product is delivered on time and within budget, and the final result meets the needs of both users and the business.

4.4 Quality Assurance and Testing: Ensuring a Reliable and Delightful User Experience

In the realm of software development, the pursuit of quality is paramount. A product may boast impressive features and innovative designs, but if it is riddled with bugs, glitches, and performance issues, it will quickly alienate users and damage the product's reputation. Quality assurance (QA) and testing are the guardians of product quality, ensuring that the software functions as intended, meets user expectations, and delivers a reliable and delightful experience.

Quality Assurance (QA): A Proactive Approach to Quality

Quality assurance is a holistic approach that encompasses a set of processes and activities designed to prevent defects and ensure that the software meets specified quality standards. QA is not just about testing; it is a proactive approach that starts early in the development cycle and continues throughout the product's lifecycle.

Key components of QA include:

- **Quality Planning:** Defining quality standards, processes, and metrics that will be used to evaluate the product.
- **Process Improvement:** Continuously analyzing and improving development processes to reduce errors and enhance efficiency.

- **Quality Control:** Monitoring and inspecting work products to ensure they adhere to established quality standards.
- **Training and Education:** Providing training to team members on quality assurance principles and practices.

Testing: Validating Functionality and Performance

Testing is a crucial part of the QA process. It involves systematically executing the software to identify defects, errors, or inconsistencies. Various testing methods are employed to assess different aspects of the product:

- **Functional Testing:** Verifying that the software functions as per the specified requirements.
- **Performance Testing:** Evaluating the software's speed, responsiveness, and stability under different loads.
- **Usability Testing:** Assessing how easy and intuitive the software is to use for the target audience.
- **Security Testing:** Identifying vulnerabilities and potential security risks in the software.
- **Compatibility Testing:** Ensuring that the software works seamlessly across different devices, operating systems, and browsers.

The Role of the Product Manager in QA and Testing:

The product manager plays a crucial role in ensuring the quality of the product. They are responsible for:

- **Defining Quality Standards:** Collaborating with stakeholders to define the quality standards that the product must meet.

- **Prioritizing QA Activities:** Working with the QA team to prioritize testing activities based on risk, impact, and available resources.
- **Reviewing Test Results:** Analyzing test results to identify defects and prioritize fixes.
- **Championing Quality:** Advocating for a culture of quality within the development team.

Best Practices for QA and Testing:

- **Start Early and Test Often:** Incorporate QA activities from the beginning of the development cycle and conduct regular testing to catch defects early.
- **Automate Testing:** Automate repetitive tests to save time and resources, and to ensure consistency in results.
- **Involve Users in Testing:** Conduct usability testing with real users to get valuable feedback on the product's design and functionality.
- **Use a Variety of Testing Methods:** Employ different testing techniques to uncover different types of defects.
- **Monitor and Measure:** Track key quality metrics to assess the effectiveness of QA efforts and identify areas for improvement.

By implementing a robust QA and testing strategy, product managers can ensure that their software products are reliable, high-performing, and user-friendly. This not only enhances customer satisfaction but also contributes to the long-term success and reputation of the product.

Product Design and Development Action List

1. **Foster Collaboration between UX/UI Designers and Developers:**
   - Define clear product requirements: Ensure designers and developers have a shared understanding of the product's goals and functionality.
   - Facilitate communication: Encourage regular communication and feedback between teams.
   - Promote a user-centered approach: Prioritize user needs and ensure designs are aligned with user expectations.
   - Manage expectations: Set realistic timelines and clearly communicate any changes or challenges.
2. **Embrace Agile Development Methodologies:**
   - Build cross-functional teams: Include members from design, development, testing, and other relevant disciplines.
   - Work in iterations (sprints): Break down the development process into shorter cycles with regular deliverables.
   - Gather continuous feedback: Seek input from stakeholders and users throughout the process to adapt and improve.
   - Prioritize working software: Focus on delivering functional features rather than excessive documentation.
   - Embrace change: Be flexible and adaptable to evolving requirements and feedback.
3. **Effectively Manage the Development Process:**
   - Create a detailed project plan: Outline tasks, timelines, milestones, and dependencies.

- Allocate resources effectively: Ensure the right people, technology, and budget are available when needed.
- Identify and mitigate risks: Proactively address potential issues that could derail the project.
- Track progress and metrics: Monitor the team's progress and identify bottlenecks or delays.
- Resolve issues promptly: Address technical, logistical, or interpersonal challenges as they arise.

4. **Implement Robust Quality Assurance (QA) and Testing:**
   - Define quality standards: Establish clear criteria for evaluating the product's functionality, performance, and user experience.
   - Plan QA activities: Determine the types of testing needed and create a testing schedule.
   - Automate testing: Use automated tools to streamline repetitive tests and improve efficiency.
   - Conduct usability testing: Gather feedback from real users to ensure the product is intuitive and user-friendly.
   - Monitor and measure: Track key quality metrics to assess progress and identify areas for improvement.

By following this action list, you can streamline your product design and development process, fostering collaboration, agility, and a commitment to quality. This will lead to the creation of successful software products that meet user needs, achieve business objectives, and stand out in the competitive market.

Chapter 5: Product Launch and Go-to-Market Strategy: Making a Grand Entrance

The culmination of countless hours of ideation, planning, design, and development is the product launch—a pivotal moment that can make or break a product's success. However, a successful launch is not merely about unveiling a finished product; it's about strategically positioning it in the market, creating awareness and excitement among your target audience, and ensuring a seamless transition from development to customer adoption.

This chapter will explore the intricate dance of product launch and go-to-market strategy, guiding you through the essential steps of introducing your product to the world and driving its adoption. We'll delve into the importance of a well-crafted marketing plan, the intricacies of building a launch strategy that aligns with your target audience, and the considerations of pricing and packaging to maximize your product's appeal. We'll also examine the various sales and distribution channels available, helping you determine the most effective ways to reach your customers.

In this chapter, you will:

- **Craft a comprehensive marketing plan:** Learn how to create a strategic roadmap for promoting your product and generating demand.
- **Develop a launch strategy:** Discover the key elements of a successful product launch, from pre-launch activities to post-launch analysis.
- **Determine optimal pricing and packaging:** Explore various pricing models and packaging options to maximize revenue and customer satisfaction.

- **Choose the right sales and distribution channels:** Identify the most effective channels for reaching your target audience and generating sales.
- **Measure and analyze launch performance:** Track key metrics and gather feedback to evaluate the success of your launch and identify areas for improvement.

By mastering the art of product launch and go-to-market strategy, you can ensure that your product makes a grand entrance, captures the attention of your target audience, and achieves lasting success in the market. This chapter will provide you with the tools, insights, and strategies to orchestrate a successful launch that sets your product on a path to sustained growth and profitability.

5.1 Creating a Marketing Plan: The Blueprint for Generating Demand

A well-crafted marketing plan is the backbone of a successful product launch. It serves as a strategic roadmap, outlining the activities, channels, and messaging that will be used to generate awareness, build excitement, and drive adoption of your product. A comprehensive marketing plan not only ensures a smooth launch but also sets the stage for long-term growth and market penetration.

Key Components of a Marketing Plan:

1. **Executive Summary:** A concise overview of the marketing plan, highlighting the key objectives, strategies, and expected outcomes.
2. **Target Audience:** A detailed description of the target customer segments, including demographics, psychographics, behaviors, and pain points. This

information should be based on thorough market research and user personas.

3. **Positioning and Messaging:** A clear articulation of the product's positioning in the market, its unique value proposition, and the key messages that will resonate with the target audience. This should be consistent across all marketing channels and materials.

4. **Marketing Goals and Objectives:** Specific, measurable, achievable, relevant, and time-bound (SMART) goals that define what the marketing plan aims to achieve. Examples include increasing brand awareness, generating leads, driving website traffic, or boosting sales.

5. **Marketing Strategies and Tactics:** A detailed outline of the marketing strategies and tactics that will be employed to achieve the marketing goals. This includes content marketing, social media marketing, email marketing, paid advertising, public relations, events, and partnerships.

6. **Marketing Budget:** A breakdown of the marketing budget, including the costs associated with each marketing activity and channel.

7. **Marketing Calendar:** A timeline that outlines the timing and sequence of marketing activities, ensuring that they are coordinated and executed effectively.

8. **Metrics and Measurement:** Key performance indicators (KPIs) that will be used to track the progress and success of the marketing plan. This includes metrics such as website traffic, lead generation, conversion rates, customer acquisition cost (CAC), and return on investment (ROI).

Developing a Marketing Plan:

1. **Conduct Market Research:** Gather data on your target audience, their needs, preferences, and behaviors. Understand the competitive landscape and identify opportunities for differentiation.
2. **Define Your Target Audience:** Based on your research, identify the specific customer segments that you will focus on.
3. **Develop Your Positioning and Messaging:** Craft a compelling value proposition and unique selling points that resonate with your target audience.
4. **Set SMART Goals:** Define clear and measurable marketing goals that align with your overall business objectives.
5. **Choose Your Marketing Channels:** Select the most effective channels for reaching your target audience. This may include a mix of online and offline channels, such as social media, email, paid advertising, public relations, events, and partnerships.
6. **Create Your Marketing Content:** Develop high-quality content that educates, informs, and engages your target audience. This could include blog posts, articles, videos, infographics, social media posts, or email newsletters.
7. **Allocate Your Budget:** Determine how much you can spend on marketing and allocate your budget across different channels and activities.
8. **Create a Marketing Calendar:** Plan the timing and sequence of your marketing activities to ensure maximum impact.
9. **Track and Measure Results:** Monitor your marketing performance using relevant KPIs and make adjustments as needed.

The Importance of Adapting Your Marketing Plan:

A marketing plan is not a static document. It should be a living, breathing document that evolves as your product and market conditions change. Regularly review and update your plan based on feedback, data, and insights to ensure that your marketing efforts remain effective and relevant.

By creating and executing a comprehensive marketing plan, you can effectively communicate the value of your product, reach your target audience, generate demand, and drive sales. A well-crafted marketing plan is essential for a successful product launch and long-term market success.

5.2 Building a Launch Strategy: Orchestrating a Successful Debut

A product launch is more than just a single event; it's a carefully orchestrated process with multiple phases, each designed to build anticipation, generate excitement, and drive adoption. A well-executed launch strategy can propel your product into the market with momentum, attracting early adopters, generating buzz, and setting the stage for long-term success.

Key Phases of a Product Launch Strategy:

1. **Pre-Launch:**
   o **Market Research and Validation:** Conduct thorough market research to validate product-market fit, identify target audience segments, and understand their needs and preferences.
   o **Positioning and Messaging:** Craft a compelling value proposition and unique selling points that differentiate your product from competitors. Develop key messages that resonate with your target audience.

- **Building Anticipation:** Generate buzz and excitement through teaser campaigns, social media engagement, content marketing, and email marketing.
- **Beta Testing:** Invite a select group of users to test the product and provide feedback. This helps to identify and address any bugs or usability issues before the official launch.
- **Preparing Marketing and Sales Materials:** Develop marketing collateral, sales presentations, and customer support resources.
- **Setting Up Distribution Channels:** Establish partnerships, secure retail placements, or prepare your online store for sales.

2. **Launch Day:**
   - **Announcement:** Make a big splash with a press release, social media posts, email blasts, or a virtual event.
   - **Media and Influencer Outreach:** Engage with media outlets and influencers to generate coverage and amplify your message.
   - **Promotions and Incentives:** Offer early-bird discounts, free trials, or other incentives to attract early adopters.
   - **Monitoring and Responding:** Closely monitor social media, online forums, and customer feedback channels to respond promptly to inquiries and address any issues.

3. **Post-Launch:**
   - **Gathering Feedback:** Collect and analyze feedback from early adopters to identify areas for improvement and inform future product iterations.

- Iterating and Improving: Make necessary changes to the product based on user feedback and data analytics.
- Scaling Marketing Efforts: Ramp up marketing and advertising to reach a wider audience and drive adoption.
- Building Community: Foster a community of users through forums, social media groups, or events to encourage engagement and advocacy.

Key Considerations for a Successful Launch:

- **Know Your Target Audience:** Tailor your launch strategy to the specific needs, preferences, and behaviors of your target audience.
- **Set Realistic Expectations:** Don't overpromise and underdeliver. Be transparent about what your product can and cannot do.
- **Be Agile and Adaptable:** Be prepared to adjust your launch strategy based on feedback, data, and market conditions.
- **Focus on the Long Term:** A successful launch is just the beginning. Focus on building a sustainable business by continuously improving your product, engaging with your customers, and expanding your market reach.

Launch Strategies for Different Types of Products:

- **Consumer Products:** Focus on generating buzz, creating a viral loop, and leveraging social media to reach a wide audience.
- **Enterprise Products:** Emphasize building relationships with key decision-makers,

demonstrating ROI, and providing comprehensive training and support.

- **SaaS Products:** Offer free trials, freemium models, or tiered pricing to attract users and encourage them to upgrade to paid plans.

By crafting a well-thought-out launch strategy and executing it with precision, you can ensure that your product makes a memorable debut, captures the attention of your target audience, and establishes a strong foundation for long-term growth and success.

5.3 Pricing and Packaging: Maximizing Value and Revenue

The pricing and packaging of your software product are critical levers that directly impact your revenue, profitability, and customer perception of value. It's a delicate balancing act—you need to set a price that reflects the value your product delivers while remaining competitive in the market and appealing to your target customers. Packaging, on the other hand, involves bundling your product's features and services in a way that caters to different customer segments and maximizes their willingness to pay.

Pricing Strategies:

There are various pricing strategies you can consider, each with its own pros and cons:

- **Cost-Plus Pricing:** This involves calculating the cost of developing and delivering your product and adding a markup to determine the selling price. It's a simple approach but may not reflect the true value customers perceive in your product.

- **Value-Based Pricing:** This strategy focuses on the perceived value your product offers to customers. It involves understanding the benefits customers derive from your product and setting a price that reflects that value.
- **Competitive Pricing:** This involves setting prices similar to or slightly lower than your competitors. It can be effective in attracting price-sensitive customers but may lead to price wars and erode profitability.
- **Skimming Pricing:** This involves setting a high initial price for your product and then gradually lowering it over time. This strategy can help you maximize revenue from early adopters but may deter price-sensitive customers.
- **Penetration Pricing:** This involves setting a low initial price to attract a large customer base and gain market share quickly. Once you have established a foothold in the market, you can gradually raise prices.
- **Freemium Pricing:** This strategy involves offering a basic version of your product for free and charging for premium features or upgrades. It can be an effective way to attract users and upsell them to paid plans.

Packaging Options:

Packaging your software product involves creating different bundles of features and services that cater to different customer segments and needs. This allows you to offer more flexibility and choice to customers, potentially increasing their willingness to pay.

Common packaging options include:

- **Tiered Pricing:** Offering different pricing tiers with varying levels of features and functionality.
- **Usage-Based Pricing:** Charging customers based on their usage of the product, such as the number of users, storage space, or API calls.
- **Per-Feature Pricing:** Allowing customers to purchase individual features or add-ons as needed.
- **Subscription-Based Pricing:** Charging customers a recurring fee for access to the product. This can provide a predictable revenue stream for the business.
- **Perpetual Licensing:** Offering customers a one-time license fee for lifetime access to the product. This can be attractive to customers who prefer to avoid recurring payments.

Choosing the Right Pricing and Packaging Strategy:

The right pricing and packaging strategy for your product will depend on various factors, including:

- **Target Market:** Understand the needs, preferences, and price sensitivity of your target customers.
- **Product Value:** Clearly articulate the value your product delivers to customers.
- **Competitive Landscape:** Analyze how your competitors are pricing and packaging their products.
- **Business Goals:** Consider your revenue goals, profitability targets, and growth objectives.

Tips for Effective Pricing and Packaging:

- **Test Different Pricing Models:** Experiment with different pricing models to see what works best for your product and target market.

- **Offer Multiple Pricing Tiers:** Give customers a choice of pricing tiers with different features and benefits.
- **Use Psychological Pricing:** Consider using pricing techniques like charm pricing (ending prices in .99) or round number pricing to influence customer perception.
- **Communicate Value Clearly:** Make sure your pricing and packaging clearly communicate the value your product delivers to customers.
- **Monitor and Adjust:** Regularly review and adjust your pricing and packaging based on customer feedback, market trends, and business performance.

By carefully considering your pricing and packaging options, you can maximize the value your product delivers to customers while also generating the revenue needed to sustain and grow your business.

5.4 Sales and Distribution Channels: Reaching Your Customers

Selecting the appropriate sales and distribution channels is paramount to the success of your product launch and long-term growth strategy. The right channels will not only help you reach your target audience effectively but also optimize your sales process and maximize revenue potential. This subchapter will explore the diverse landscape of sales and distribution channels available for software products, helping you choose the most suitable options for your specific product and target market.

Direct Sales Channels:

- **In-House Sales Team:** This involves building and managing your own sales team to directly engage with potential customers. It offers greater control over the sales process and allows for personalized interactions, but it can be costly and time-consuming to build and maintain an effective sales force.

- **Online Sales (Website or App):** This involves selling your product directly through your website or a dedicated mobile app. It provides a convenient and accessible way for customers to purchase your product, but it requires a robust online presence and effective digital marketing strategies.

Indirect Sales Channels:

- **Resellers and Distributors:** These are third-party companies that purchase your product in bulk and then resell it to their own customers. This can help you expand your reach and tap into new markets, but it also means sharing a portion of your revenue with the reseller.
- **Affiliate Marketing:** This involves partnering with other businesses or individuals (affiliates) who promote your product in exchange for a commission on each sale. It's a cost-effective way to expand your reach, but it requires careful management to ensure the affiliates are representing your brand accurately.
- **App Stores (Mobile Apps):** If your product is a mobile app, listing it on popular app stores like Apple's App Store or Google Play can give you access to a vast audience of potential users. However, it also means adhering to the platform's rules and sharing a portion of your revenue.
- **Cloud Marketplaces (SaaS):** For cloud-based software (SaaS), listing your product on platforms like AWS Marketplace or Azure Marketplace can

expose it to a large pool of potential customers already using those cloud services.

Hybrid Sales Channels:

Many companies opt for a hybrid approach, combining direct and indirect sales channels to maximize their reach and leverage the strengths of each channel. For example, you could have an in-house sales team for high-value enterprise deals, while using resellers to reach smaller businesses or consumers.

Choosing the Right Channels:

Selecting the most suitable sales and distribution channels depends on various factors:

- **Target Audience:** Where do your target customers typically look for and purchase software products?
- **Product Type:** Is your product a consumer app, enterprise software, or a specialized tool?
- **Pricing Strategy:** Does your pricing model align with the typical commission structures of resellers or app stores?
- **Resources:** Do you have the resources to build and manage an in-house sales team?
- **Market Maturity:** Is your market well-established, or are you trying to break into a new market?

It's crucial to research and analyze different channels to determine which ones are the most appropriate for your product and target audience. Consider factors like reach, cost, control, and alignment with your overall business strategy.

By strategically selecting and managing your sales and distribution channels, you can effectively reach your target customers, optimize your sales process, and drive revenue growth for your software product.

Product Launch and Go-to-Market Strategy Action List

1. **Develop a Comprehensive Marketing Plan:**
   - Conduct thorough market research: Understand your target audience, their needs, and the competitive landscape.
   - Define your target audience: Identify specific customer segments you want to reach.
   - Craft your positioning and messaging: Develop a clear value proposition and unique selling points that resonate with your audience.
   - Set SMART goals: Establish specific, measurable, achievable, relevant, and time-bound marketing objectives.
   - Choose your marketing channels: Select the most effective channels for reaching your target audience (e.g., social media, email, paid advertising, PR, events).
   - Create engaging content: Develop high-quality content that educates, informs, and entertains your audience.
   - Allocate your budget: Determine your marketing spend and distribute it across channels and activities.
   - Create a marketing calendar: Plan the timing and sequence of your marketing activities.

- Track and measure results: Monitor key performance indicators (KPIs) to assess the effectiveness of your campaigns.
2. **Build a Robust Launch Strategy:**
   - Validate product-market fit: Ensure your product meets a genuine need in the market.
   - Build anticipation: Generate buzz and excitement before launch through teasers and early access programs.
   - Plan your launch event: Create a memorable experience that showcases your product's value.
   - Leverage media and influencers: Partner with media outlets and influencers to amplify your message.
   - Offer promotions and incentives: Attract early adopters with discounts, free trials, or other special offers.
   - Monitor and respond to feedback: Engage with customers and address any questions or concerns promptly.
3. **Determine Optimal Pricing and Packaging:**
   - Analyze your costs: Understand the cost of developing, producing, and delivering your product.
   - Research the market: Assess competitor pricing and customer expectations.
   - Consider different pricing models: Explore options like cost-plus, value-based, competitive, skimming, penetration, freemium, or subscription-based pricing.
   - Offer multiple pricing tiers: Cater to different customer segments with varying needs and budgets.

- Communicate value clearly: Ensure your pricing reflects the value your product provides.
- Monitor and adjust: Continuously review your pricing based on market feedback and performance.

4. **Select the Right Sales and Distribution Channels:**
   - Analyze your target audience: Determine where your customers are most likely to discover and purchase your product.
   - Consider your product type: Choose channels that are appropriate for your specific product (e.g., app stores for mobile apps, cloud marketplaces for SaaS).
   - Evaluate direct and indirect options: Assess the benefits and drawbacks of in-house sales teams, resellers, affiliates, app stores, and cloud marketplaces.
   - Build a hybrid approach: Combine different channels to maximize your reach and revenue potential.

5. **Measure and Analyze Launch Performance:**
   - Track key metrics: Monitor sales, website traffic, user engagement, customer acquisition cost (CAC), and other relevant KPIs.
   - Gather feedback: Collect customer reviews, conduct surveys, and analyze social media mentions to understand user sentiment.
   - Iterate and improve: Use data and insights to refine your marketing, sales, and product strategies.

By implementing this action list, you can develop a comprehensive go-to-market strategy that ensures your product launch is a success and sets the stage for continued growth and profitability in the market.

Chapter 6: Measuring and Optimizing Product Success: The Data-Driven Path to Continuous Improvement

Launching a product is a significant milestone, but the journey doesn't end there. In the dynamic and competitive world of software, sustained success hinges on your ability to measure, analyze, and optimize your product's performance. This chapter delves into the critical practice of data-driven product management, where insights gleaned from user behavior, market trends, and key performance indicators (KPIs) guide your decision-making and fuel continuous product improvement.

The era of relying solely on intuition and gut feeling is long gone. Today, successful product managers harness the power of data to gain a deeper understanding of their users, identify areas for improvement, and make informed decisions that drive product growth and profitability. By measuring and analyzing key metrics, you can uncover hidden patterns, validate assumptions, and make data-driven adjustments to your product roadmap, marketing strategies, and overall business approach.

In this chapter, you will:

- **Define Key Performance Indicators (KPIs):** Identify the most relevant metrics that measure the success of your product and align with your business goals.
- **Implement Analytics and Tracking:** Learn how to set up tracking mechanisms to collect data on user behavior, engagement, and conversion.
- **Analyze Data and Make Data-Driven Decisions:** Discover techniques for extracting meaningful

insights from data and using them to inform product decisions.

- **Iterate and Improve the Product:** Embrace a culture of continuous improvement, using data-driven feedback to refine your product and enhance the user experience.

By mastering the art of measuring and optimizing product success, you'll be equipped to navigate the complexities of the market, stay ahead of the competition, and deliver a product that truly resonates with your target audience. This chapter will empower you with the knowledge and tools to make data-driven decisions that drive growth, increase customer satisfaction, and ensure the long-term success of your product.

6.1 Defining Key Performance Indicators (KPIs): Measuring What Matters

Key Performance Indicators (KPIs) are the quantifiable metrics that provide valuable insights into the health and success of your software product. They act as a compass, guiding your decision-making and revealing areas that require attention or optimization. However, not all metrics are created equal. Choosing the right KPIs is crucial for focusing your efforts on the aspects that truly matter for your product's growth and profitability.

Types of KPIs:

KPIs can be categorized into various types, each addressing different aspects of your product and business:

1. **User Engagement KPIs:** These metrics measure how users interact with your product. Examples include:

- **Active Users:** The number of users who engage with your product within a specific time frame.
- **Session Duration:** The average length of time users spend in a single session.
- **Retention Rate:** The percentage of users who return to your product after a certain period.
- **Churn Rate:** The percentage of users who stop using your product.

2. **Revenue KPIs:** These metrics assess your product's financial performance. Examples include:
   - **Monthly Recurring Revenue (MRR):** The predictable revenue generated by your product each month.
   - **Average Revenue Per User (ARPU):** The average revenue generated per user.
   - **Customer Lifetime Value (LTV):** The total revenue a customer generates over their entire relationship with your product.
   - **Customer Acquisition Cost (CAC):** The cost of acquiring a new customer.

3. **Conversion KPIs:** These metrics track how effectively your product converts users into paying customers. Examples include:
   - **Conversion Rate:** The percentage of users who complete a desired action, such as signing up for a trial or making a purchase.
   - **Time to Conversion:** The average time it takes for a user to convert into a paying customer.

4. **Customer Satisfaction KPIs:** These metrics measure how satisfied customers are with your product. Examples include:

- o **Net Promoter Score (NPS):** A measure of customer loyalty and willingness to recommend your product.
- o **Customer Satisfaction Score (CSAT):** A measure of customer satisfaction with specific interactions or features.
5. **Operational KPIs:** These metrics assess the efficiency and effectiveness of your product's development and delivery processes. Examples include:
    - o **Cycle Time:** The time it takes to complete a task or feature.
    - o **Lead Time:** The time it takes from the initial customer request to the delivery of the feature.
    - o **Defect Density:** The number of defects per unit of code.

Choosing the Right KPIs:

The KPIs you choose should be aligned with your overall product strategy and business goals. Here are some tips for selecting the right KPIs:

- **Start with your business objectives:** What are you trying to achieve with your product? What are the most important metrics that will indicate your progress towards those objectives?
- **Consider your stage of development:** The KPIs that are relevant for a new product may be different from those for a mature product.
- **Focus on actionable metrics:** Choose KPIs that you can influence and that will provide insights that you can act upon.
- **Limit the number of KPIs:** Too many KPIs can be overwhelming and distracting. Focus on the most

critical metrics that will give you the most valuable insights.

Measuring KPIs:

Once you have defined your KPIs, you need to establish a system for tracking and measuring them. This may involve implementing analytics tools, setting up dashboards, or conducting regular surveys.

Analyzing and Acting on KPIs:

KPIs are not just numbers; they are a source of valuable insights. Regularly analyze your KPIs to identify trends, understand user behavior, and uncover opportunities for improvement. Use your findings to inform your product roadmap, marketing strategies, and overall business approach.

By defining and tracking the right KPIs, you can gain a deeper understanding of your product's performance, make data-driven decisions, and continuously improve your product to meet the evolving needs of your customers.

6.2 Implementing Analytics and Tracking: Harnessing the Power of Data

While defining the right Key Performance Indicators (KPIs) is crucial, the true power of data-driven decision-making lies in your ability to effectively collect, track, and analyze the data that fuels those KPIs. This subchapter will explore the world of analytics and tracking tools, guiding you through the process of setting up robust tracking mechanisms to capture valuable insights into user behavior, engagement, and conversion.

Understanding Analytics and Tracking Tools

Analytics and tracking tools are software platforms designed to collect, process, and visualize data about user interactions with your product. They provide a wealth of information, from basic usage statistics (like page views and clicks) to more complex behavioral data (like user journeys and conversion funnels).

Key features of analytics and tracking tools:

- **Data Collection:** These tools use various methods to collect data, such as website tags, mobile SDKs, and server-side logging.
- **Data Processing:** The collected data is cleaned, aggregated, and transformed into a usable format.
- **Data Visualization:** The processed data is presented in visually appealing and easy-to-understand dashboards, reports, and charts.
- **Customizable Reports:** Most tools allow you to create custom reports and dashboards to track the specific metrics that are most important to you.
- **Segmentation:** Many tools offer segmentation capabilities, allowing you to analyze data for specific user groups or cohorts.
- **Goal Tracking:** You can set up goals to track conversions and other key events.
- **A/B Testing:** Some tools enable you to run experiments to test different variations of your product and measure their impact on user behavior.

Popular Analytics and Tracking Tools:

- **Google Analytics:** A widely used web analytics platform that offers a comprehensive set of features for tracking website traffic and user behavior.

- **Mixpanel:** A product analytics platform that focuses on tracking user interactions and events within your product.
- **Amplitude:** A product intelligence platform that helps you understand user behavior, identify growth opportunities, and optimize your product.
- **Heap:** A behavioral analytics platform that automatically captures all user interactions, allowing you to analyze user behavior without writing any code.

Implementing Analytics and Tracking:

1. **Choose the Right Tools:** Select the tools that best suit your needs and budget. Consider factors such as the type of data you want to collect, the features you need, and the ease of implementation.
2. **Define Your Tracking Plan:** Determine what data you want to collect and how you will use it. This will help you to set up your tracking correctly and ensure that you are collecting the most relevant data.
3. **Implement Tracking Code:** Add the necessary tracking code to your website, mobile app, or product. This may involve working with your development team.
4. **Set Up Goals and Events:** Define the key actions or events that you want to track, such as signups, purchases, or feature usage.
5. **Create Custom Reports and Dashboards:** Customize your analytics reports and dashboards to focus on the metrics that are most important to you.
6. **Monitor and Analyze Data:** Regularly review your data to identify trends, understand user behavior, and make data-driven decisions.

Tips for Effective Analytics and Tracking:

- **Start with the Basics:** Don't try to track everything at once. Start with the most important metrics and gradually add more as needed.
- **Ensure Data Accuracy:** Make sure your tracking is implemented correctly and that the data you are collecting is accurate and reliable.
- **Focus on Actionable Insights:** Don't just collect data for the sake of it. Use your data to identify actionable insights that can help you improve your product.
- **Experiment and Iterate:** Use your data to test hypotheses and experiment with different approaches.

By implementing effective analytics and tracking, you can gain a deeper understanding of your users, measure the success of your product, and make data-driven decisions that drive growth and profitability.

6.3 Analyzing Data and Making Data-Driven Decisions: Turning Insights into Action

Collecting data is just the first step. The true value of analytics lies in the ability to analyze that data and extract meaningful insights that inform product decisions and drive improvement. This subchapter will explore the process of data analysis and the art of making data-driven decisions, helping you transform raw data into actionable strategies for product success.

Understanding Data Analysis

Data analysis is the process of inspecting, cleaning, transforming, and modeling data to discover useful information, inform conclusions, and support decision-making. It involves using various statistical and analytical techniques to identify patterns, trends, correlations, and anomalies in your data.

Key aspects of data analysis:

- **Data Cleaning:** This involves identifying and correcting errors, inconsistencies, or missing values in your data.
- **Exploratory Data Analysis (EDA):** This involves summarizing the main characteristics of your data through visualizations and descriptive statistics.
- **Confirmatory Data Analysis (CDA):** This involves testing hypotheses and drawing conclusions about your data using statistical methods.
- **Predictive Analytics:** This involves using historical data to predict future trends or outcomes.
- **Prescriptive Analytics:** This involves using data to recommend actions or decisions.

Tools for Data Analysis:

There are various tools available for data analysis, ranging from simple spreadsheets to sophisticated data science platforms. Some popular tools include:

- **Excel/Google Sheets:** These ubiquitous spreadsheet tools can be used for basic data analysis and visualization.
- **SQL:** This powerful query language is used to retrieve and manipulate data from relational databases.

- **Python/R:** These programming languages are popular for data analysis and machine learning due to their extensive libraries and frameworks.
- **Tableau/Power BI:** These business intelligence platforms offer powerful visualization and dashboarding capabilities.

Making Data-Driven Decisions:

Data-driven decision-making (DDDM) is the practice of basing strategic business decisions on data analysis and interpretation. It involves using data to:

- **Validate assumptions:** Test hypotheses and assumptions about user behavior and product performance.
- **Identify problems and opportunities:** Uncover issues that need to be addressed or opportunities that can be exploited.
- **Prioritize initiatives:** Focus resources on the initiatives that are most likely to have the biggest impact.
- **Measure progress:** Track the progress of your product and initiatives over time.
- **Make adjustments:** Continually refine your product roadmap, marketing strategies, and overall business approach based on data-driven feedback.

Tips for Making Data-Driven Decisions:

- **Start with a question:** What do you want to learn from your data? What decisions are you trying to inform?
- **Choose the right metrics:** What are the most relevant KPIs for answering your question?

- **Collect and clean your data:** Ensure that your data is accurate and reliable.
- **Analyze your data:** Use appropriate analytical techniques to explore and interpret your data.
- **Draw conclusions and make recommendations:** Based on your analysis, what conclusions can you draw? What recommendations can you make?
- **Communicate your findings:** Share your insights with stakeholders in a clear and concise manner.

Challenges of Data-Driven Decision-Making:

- **Data Quality:** Poor data quality can lead to inaccurate or misleading conclusions.
- **Data Bias:** Data can be biased, either intentionally or unintentionally.
- **Data Overload:** Too much data can be overwhelming and make it difficult to identify meaningful insights.
- **Analysis Paralysis:** Overthinking or overanalyzing data can lead to inaction.

By overcoming these challenges and embracing a data-driven approach, product managers can unlock the power of data to make better decisions, drive product success, and achieve their business goals.

6.4 Iterating and Improving the Product: The Cycle of Continuous Enhancement

In the ever-evolving landscape of software, stagnation is not an option. The most successful products are those that continuously evolve and adapt to meet the changing needs and expectations of users. This process of iteration and improvement is a fundamental pillar of product management, ensuring that your product remains relevant, competitive, and delivers ongoing value to your customers.

The Iteration Cycle:

Product iteration is a cyclical process that involves:

1. **Gathering Feedback:** Collect feedback from users, stakeholders, and data analytics to identify areas for improvement. This can be done through surveys, interviews, user testing, and analyzing usage data.
2. **Prioritizing Improvements:** Based on the feedback received, prioritize the improvements that will have the most significant impact on user satisfaction, business goals, and product performance.
3. **Planning and Implementing:** Develop a plan for implementing the selected improvements, including timelines, resources, and success metrics.
4. **Testing and Validating:** Thoroughly test the implemented changes to ensure they work as expected and do not introduce new issues.
5. **Releasing and Monitoring:** Release the updated product to users and monitor its performance using relevant KPIs.
6. **Repeat:** The cycle begins anew, with continuous feedback collection and analysis driving further iterations and improvements.

Benefits of Iterative Product Development:

- **Reduced Risk:** By releasing smaller, incremental updates, you can test new features and ideas with a smaller group of users, reducing the risk of major failures.

- **Faster Time to Market:** Iterative development allows you to get new features and improvements into the hands of users more quickly, accelerating the learning process.
- **Improved Customer Satisfaction:** By constantly listening to feedback and making improvements, you can ensure that your product meets the evolving needs of your customers.
- **Increased Adaptability:** Iterative development allows you to respond quickly to changes in the market or competitive landscape.
- **Enhanced Team Morale:** Seeing the product improve and evolve over time can boost team morale and motivation.

Challenges of Iterative Product Development:

- **Scope Creep:** It can be tempting to add more and more features to each iteration, leading to scope creep and delays. It's important to maintain focus and prioritize the most impactful improvements.
- **Technical Debt:** Rapid iterations can sometimes lead to accumulating technical debt, which is the implied cost of additional rework caused by choosing an easy solution now instead of using a better approach that would take longer. It's important to allocate time for refactoring and code improvement to keep technical debt under control.
- **Communication Overhead:** Frequent releases and changes can require significant communication and coordination with stakeholders to manage expectations and ensure alignment.

Best Practices for Iterative Product Development:

- **Set Clear Goals for Each Iteration:** Define specific objectives for each iteration, focusing on delivering value to customers and achieving business goals.
- **Prioritize Ruthlessly:** Focus on the most impactful improvements that will have the biggest impact on user satisfaction and business outcomes.
- **Test and Validate Early and Often:** Don't wait until the end of the development cycle to test new features. Get feedback from users early and often to identify and address issues before they become major problems.
- **Monitor and Measure:** Track key metrics to assess the impact of each iteration and identify areas for further improvement.
- **Embrace Failure:** Not every iteration will be a success. Learn from your mistakes and use them to improve your process.

By embracing an iterative approach to product development, you can create a culture of continuous improvement, deliver value to customers more frequently, and build a product that adapts and thrives in a constantly changing market.

Measuring and Optimizing Product Success Action List

1. **Define Key Performance Indicators (KPIs):**
   - Align with business objectives: Choose KPIs that reflect your overall product strategy and business goals.
   - Consider your stage of development: Tailor KPIs to your product's maturity level (e.g., focus on user acquisition for new products, retention for mature products).

- Prioritize actionable metrics: Select KPIs that you can influence and that provide insights you can act upon.
- Limit the number of KPIs: Focus on the most critical metrics to avoid information overload.

2. **Implement Analytics and Tracking:**
   - Choose the right tools: Select analytics platforms that align with your needs and budget (e.g., Google Analytics, Mixpanel, Amplitude, Heap).
   - Create a tracking plan: Define what data you want to collect, how you'll collect it, and how you'll use it.
   - Implement tracking code: Work with your development team to add tracking code to your website, app, or product.
   - Set up goals and events: Define key actions or events you want to track (e.g., signups, purchases, feature usage).
   - Build custom reports and dashboards: Tailor your analytics views to focus on the most relevant metrics.

3. **Analyze Data and Make Data-Driven Decisions:**
   - Clean and prepare data: Ensure your data is accurate and free of errors or inconsistencies.
   - Explore and visualize data: Use charts, graphs, and other visualizations to identify patterns and trends.
   - Apply statistical methods: Use appropriate techniques to test hypotheses and draw conclusions from your data.
   - Identify actionable insights: Look for patterns, correlations, and anomalies that suggest areas for improvement.

o Validate assumptions: Use data to test your hypotheses about user behavior and product performance.
o Prioritize initiatives: Focus your resources on the changes that will have the most significant impact.

4. **Iterate and Improve the Product:**
    o Gather feedback: Collect feedback from users, stakeholders, and data analytics to identify areas for improvement.
    o Prioritize improvements: Focus on the most impactful changes based on feedback and data analysis.
    o Plan and implement changes: Develop a plan for implementing improvements, including timelines, resources, and success metrics.
    o Test and validate changes: Thoroughly test all changes before releasing them to users.
    o Release and monitor: Deploy updates and monitor their impact using relevant KPIs.
    o Repeat the cycle: Continuously gather feedback, analyze data, and iterate on your product to ensure ongoing improvement and customer satisfaction.

By implementing this action list, you can establish a robust framework for measuring and optimizing your product's success. This data-driven approach will empower you to make informed decisions, enhance the user experience, and drive continuous growth and improvement for your product.

Part III: Advanced Topics in Software Product Management

Chapter 7: Product Management in Different Contexts: Adapting Your Approach for Success

The role of the product manager is not a one-size-fits-all proposition. It can vary significantly depending on the specific context in which you operate. The type of product, the target market, the company size and structure, and the industry landscape all play a crucial role in shaping the challenges, opportunities, and strategies that product managers must employ.

In this chapter, we will explore the nuances of product management in different contexts, examining how the role adapts to the specific demands of various scenarios. We will delve into the contrasting dynamics of B2B (business-to-business) and B2C (business-to-consumer) product management, highlighting the differences in customer needs, decision-making processes, and marketing strategies. We will also examine the unique challenges and opportunities faced by product managers in startups versus established enterprises, where resources, processes, and risk tolerance can vary significantly.

Additionally, we will explore the distinct characteristics of SaaS (Software-as-a-Service) products compared to traditional on-premise software, addressing the implications for pricing, deployment, customer support, and product updates. By understanding the nuances of these different contexts, you will be better equipped to tailor your approach, adapt your strategies, and ultimately achieve success in your chosen product management path.

In this chapter, you will:

- **Understand the differences between B2B and B2C product management:** Learn how to tailor your approach to the specific needs and expectations of business customers versus individual consumers.
- **Navigate the challenges and opportunities of product management in startups and enterprises:** Discover strategies for balancing agility and innovation with the need for structure and scalability.
- **Master the unique aspects of SaaS product management:** Learn how to leverage the cloud-based delivery model to create flexible, scalable, and customer-centric software solutions.

By understanding the unique challenges and opportunities presented by different contexts, you can develop a versatile skillset that enables you to thrive as a product manager in any environment. This chapter will provide you with the insights and strategies needed to adapt your approach, navigate diverse scenarios, and ultimately achieve product success, regardless of the context.

7.1 B2B vs. B2C: Contrasting Landscapes, Divergent Approaches

While the core principles of product management remain consistent across different contexts, the strategies and tactics employed by product managers can vary significantly depending on whether they are working on a B2B (business-to-business) or B2C (business-to-consumer) product. Understanding the nuances of these two distinct markets is crucial for tailoring your approach and achieving success in your chosen domain.

B2B Product Management: Serving the Needs of Businesses

In the B2B realm, your customers are other businesses or organizations. They are typically seeking solutions that can help them improve efficiency, reduce costs, increase revenue, or gain a competitive edge. B2B products are often complex, requiring extensive customization and integration with existing systems.

Key characteristics of B2B product management:

- **Customers:** Businesses or organizations of varying sizes, from small startups to large enterprises.
- **Decision-Making:** Involves multiple stakeholders, often with complex buying processes and longer sales cycles.
- **Value Proposition:** Focused on demonstrating a clear return on investment (ROI) and addressing specific business needs.
- **Marketing and Sales:** Emphasizes building relationships, providing personalized solutions, and demonstrating expertise.
- **Pricing:** Often involves complex pricing models, such as tiered pricing, volume discounts, or custom quotes.

B2B product managers need to be skilled at:

- **Understanding complex business needs:** Identifying the pain points and challenges faced by businesses and translating them into product requirements.

- **Building relationships with key stakeholders:** Engaging with decision-makers, influencers, and end-users to gain buy-in and ensure successful adoption.
- **Managing complex sales cycles:** Navigating lengthy sales processes that involve multiple stakeholders and require building consensus.
- **Demonstrating ROI:** Quantifying the value that the product delivers to the business in terms of increased revenue, reduced costs, or improved efficiency.

B2C Product Management: Delighting Individual Consumers

In the B2C world, your customers are individual consumers who are seeking products or services to enhance their personal lives, solve everyday problems, or fulfill their desires. B2C products are often designed for mass appeal, focusing on ease of use, emotional connection, and brand experience.

Key characteristics of B2C product management:

- **Customers:** Individual consumers with diverse demographics, interests, and preferences.
- **Decision-Making:** Often involves individual or household decision-makers with shorter sales cycles and simpler buying processes.
- **Value Proposition:** Focused on delivering personal benefits, emotional satisfaction, and a positive brand experience.

- **Marketing and Sales:** Emphasizes mass-market appeal, emotional branding, and creating a sense of urgency or desire.
- **Pricing:** Typically involves simpler pricing models, such as fixed prices or subscription fees.

B2C product managers need to be skilled at:

- **Understanding consumer behavior:** Identifying the needs, desires, and pain points of individual consumers and translating them into product features and benefits.
- **Creating emotional connections:** Developing marketing messages and product experiences that resonate with consumers on an emotional level.
- **Driving rapid adoption:** Launching products quickly and generating buzz to capture market share.
- **Managing customer feedback:** Monitoring and responding to customer feedback to continuously improve the product and user experience.

Key Differences: B2B vs. B2C Product Management

Aspect	B2B	B2C
Customers	Businesses or organizations	Individual consumers
Decision-Making	Multiple stakeholders, complex buying process, longer sales cycles	Individual or household decision-makers, shorter sales cycles
Value Proposition	ROI, business needs	Personal benefits, emotional satisfaction, brand experience
Marketing and Sales	Relationship building, personalized solutions, expertise	Mass-market appeal, emotional branding, creating urgency/desire
Pricing	Complex pricing models	Simpler pricing models

By understanding the key differences between B2B and B2C product management, you can tailor your approach to the specific context, build effective strategies, and deliver products that meet the unique needs and expectations of your target market. Whether you're developing software for businesses or consumers, a deep understanding of your audience is crucial for achieving product success.

7.2 Startups vs. Enterprises: Navigating Different Worlds of Product Management

The experience of a product manager in a nimble startup can be vastly different from that in a large, established enterprise. Each environment presents unique challenges and opportunities, requiring different skill sets, strategies, and approaches. Understanding these differences is crucial for adapting your product management style and maximizing your impact in either setting.

Startups: Embracing Agility and Innovation

Startups are characterized by their fast-paced, dynamic, and often resource-constrained environments. They are driven by a strong entrepreneurial spirit, a focus on rapid innovation, and a desire to disrupt the market.

Key characteristics of product management in startups:

- **Limited Resources:** Startups often have limited funding, manpower, and time. Product managers must be resourceful and prioritize ruthlessly, focusing on the most impactful features and initiatives.
- **High Uncertainty:** The market landscape for startups can be uncertain and rapidly changing. Product managers must be adaptable and willing to pivot their strategies based on new information and feedback.
- **Strong Customer Focus:** Early customer adoption and feedback are crucial for startup success. Product managers must engage closely with early users, gather feedback, and iterate quickly to build a product that meets market needs.
- **Wearing Multiple Hats:** In small startups, product managers often wear multiple hats, taking on responsibilities that might be handled by separate teams in larger organizations. This requires a broad skill set and the ability to juggle multiple priorities.

Challenges in startup product management:

- **Resource Constraints:** Balancing limited resources with the need to build a high-quality product.
- **Market Uncertainty:** Navigating an uncertain market and adapting to changing conditions.
- **Building a Team:** Attracting and retaining top talent in a competitive environment.
- **Establishing Processes:** Creating scalable processes and structures as the company grows.

Opportunities in startup product management:

- **Greater Impact:** Product managers in startups have the opportunity to make a significant impact on the product and the company's direction.
- **Faster Decision-Making:** Startups often have a flatter hierarchy, allowing for quicker decision-making and faster implementation of new ideas.
- **Learning and Growth:** The fast-paced and dynamic environment of a startup provides ample opportunities for learning and professional growth.

Enterprises: Scaling for Growth and Stability

Enterprises are large, established organizations with significant resources, complex structures, and established processes. They often have a strong focus on stability, efficiency, and maintaining their market position.

Key characteristics of product management in enterprises:

- **Abundant Resources:** Enterprises typically have access to more resources, including funding, manpower, and technology. This allows for larger-scale projects and more comprehensive product development efforts.

- **Established Processes:** Enterprises often have well-defined processes and procedures for product development, which can provide structure and predictability.
- **Multiple Stakeholders:** Product managers in enterprises must navigate a complex network of stakeholders, including executives, department heads, and cross-functional teams.
- **Slower Decision-Making:** The decision-making process in enterprises can be slow and bureaucratic due to the need for consensus and approval from multiple stakeholders.

Challenges in enterprise product management:

- **Bureaucracy:** Navigating complex organizational structures and decision-making processes.
- **Innovation:** Fostering innovation in a large, established organization.
- **Prioritization:** Balancing the needs of different stakeholders and competing priorities.
- **Communication:** Effectively communicating the product vision and strategy across a large organization.

Opportunities in enterprise product management:

- **Scale and Impact:** Product managers in enterprises have the opportunity to impact a large number of users and drive significant business results.
- **Resources and Expertise:** Enterprises have access to a wealth of resources and expertise, which can be leveraged to develop high-quality products.
- **Career Growth:** There are often clear career paths and opportunities for advancement within large organizations.

By understanding the unique dynamics of startups and enterprises, you can adapt your product management style to the specific context and thrive in either environment. Whether you're driven by the fast-paced innovation of a startup or the scale and impact of an enterprise, a successful product manager knows how to navigate the specific challenges and leverage the opportunities presented by each setting.

7.3 SaaS vs. On-Premise Software: Embracing the Cloud and Beyond

The choice between Software-as-a-Service (SaaS) and on-premise software deployment models has a profound impact on the strategies and considerations for product managers. Each model presents unique advantages and challenges, requiring different approaches to development, delivery, pricing, and customer support. Understanding the nuances of these two models is essential for tailoring your product management approach to meet the specific demands of your chosen path.

SaaS (Software-as-a-Service): The Cloud-Powered Paradigm

SaaS is a software delivery model where applications are hosted on remote servers and accessed by users over the internet. It eliminates the need for users to install and maintain the software on their own infrastructure, offering a convenient, flexible, and scalable solution.

Key characteristics of SaaS product management:

- **Delivery Model:** Hosted on remote servers and accessed via the internet.

- **Pricing:** Typically subscription-based, with monthly or annual fees.
- **Deployment:** Quick and easy, with minimal setup required on the user's end.
- **Updates and Maintenance:** Handled by the provider, ensuring users always have the latest version.
- **Accessibility:** Accessible from any device with an internet connection.
- **Scalability:** Easily scalable to accommodate changing user needs.

SaaS product managers need to be skilled at:

- **Customer Acquisition and Retention:** SaaS businesses rely heavily on customer acquisition and retention. Product managers need to focus on driving signups, onboarding new users effectively, and minimizing churn.
- **Pricing and Packaging:** Developing flexible pricing models and packaging options that cater to different customer segments and needs.
- **Customer Support:** Providing excellent customer support to ensure user satisfaction and minimize churn.
- **Data Analytics:** Leveraging usage data to understand customer behavior, identify areas for improvement, and drive product evolution.
- **Continuous Delivery:** Adopting a continuous delivery model to release new features and updates frequently and seamlessly.

On-Premise Software: The Traditional Approach

On-premise software is installed and run on computers on the premises of the person or organization using the software, rather than at a remote facility such as a server farm or cloud.

Key characteristics of on-premise product management:

- **Delivery Model:** Software is installed and run on the user's own infrastructure.
- **Pricing:** Typically a one-time license fee or perpetual license.
- **Deployment:** Can be complex and time-consuming, requiring IT expertise.
- **Updates and Maintenance:** Responsibility of the user, often requiring manual updates and patches.
- **Accessibility:** Limited to the devices where the software is installed.
- **Scalability:** Can be less flexible and may require additional hardware investments for scaling.

On-premise product managers need to be skilled at:

- **Understanding Customer Requirements:** Gathering detailed requirements from customers to ensure the software meets their specific needs.
- **Managing Complex Deployments:** Coordinating the installation and configuration of the software on the customer's infrastructure.
- **Providing Technical Support:** Offering robust technical support to address any issues or problems that arise.
- **Managing Upgrades and Updates:** Planning and executing software upgrades and updates to ensure compatibility and security.
- **Long-Term Customer Relationships:** Building strong relationships with customers to ensure their continued satisfaction and loyalty.

Choosing the Right Model:

The choice between SaaS and on-premise software depends on various factors, including:

- **Target Market:** The needs and preferences of your target customers.
- **Product Complexity:** Simple products may be better suited for SaaS, while complex products may require the customization and control offered by on-premise solutions.
- **Cost:** SaaS typically has lower upfront costs, while on-premise software may have higher initial costs but lower ongoing costs.
- **Control and Customization:** On-premise software offers greater control and customization options, while SaaS is generally more standardized.

By understanding the unique characteristics of SaaS and on-premise software, you can choose the deployment model that best aligns with your product strategy, target market, and business goals. Whether you embrace the cloud-powered flexibility of SaaS or the customization and control of on-premise solutions, the key is to leverage the strengths of each model to deliver a product that meets the needs of your customers and drives your business forward.

Product Management in Different Contexts Action List

1. **B2B vs. B2C:**

- **Understand your customers:**
    - ○ B2B: Research the needs and pain points of businesses or organizations.

- **B2C:** Analyze the desires, preferences, and behaviors of individual consumers.
- **Tailor your value proposition:**
  - **B2B:** Focus on demonstrating ROI and addressing specific business needs.
  - **B2C:** Emphasize personal benefits, emotional satisfaction, and a positive brand experience.
- **Adapt your marketing and sales strategies:**
  - **B2B:** Prioritize relationship building, personalized solutions, and demonstrating expertise.
  - **B2C:** Focus on mass-market appeal, emotional branding, and creating a sense of urgency or desire.
- **Choose the right pricing model:**
  - **B2B:** Consider complex pricing models like tiered pricing, volume discounts, or custom quotes.
  - **B2C:** Opt for simpler pricing models like fixed prices or subscription fees.

2. **Startups vs. Enterprises:**

- **Assess your resources:**
  - Startups: Prioritize ruthlessly and focus on the most impactful features and initiatives.
  - Enterprises: Leverage your resources to develop comprehensive and scalable solutions.
- **Manage your environment:**
  - Startups: Embrace agility and adaptability, be prepared to pivot based on feedback and data.

- o Enterprises: Navigate complex organizational structures and build consensus among stakeholders.
- **Optimize your decision-making:**
  - o Startups: Take advantage of faster decision-making processes to implement new ideas quickly.
  - o Enterprises: Foster a culture of innovation and empower teams to take calculated risks.

3. **SaaS vs. On-Premise Software:**

- **Choose the right delivery model:**
  - o SaaS: Focus on customer acquisition and retention, flexible pricing, excellent customer support, data analytics, and continuous delivery.
  - o On-Premise: Prioritize understanding customer requirements, managing complex deployments, providing technical support, managing upgrades, and building long-term relationships.
- **Tailor your pricing strategy:**
  - o SaaS: Consider subscription-based pricing or tiered pricing models.
  - o On-Premise: Offer one-time license fees or perpetual licenses.
- **Manage customer expectations:**
  - o SaaS: Communicate the benefits of cloud-based access, regular updates, and scalability.
  - o On-Premise: Highlight the control, customization options, and potential long-term cost savings.

By following this action list, you can tailor your product management approach to the specific context of your product, company, and target market, increasing your chances of success in diverse environments.

Chapter 8: Emerging Trends in Software Product Management: Navigating the Future of Innovation

The world of software product management is in a constant state of flux, driven by rapid technological advancements, shifting customer expectations, and evolving market dynamics. Staying ahead of the curve requires not only a deep understanding of current best practices but also a keen eye on the horizon, anticipating the trends that will shape the future of product development and delivery.

This chapter will explore the most promising and impactful emerging trends in software product management, delving into how they are reshaping the role of the product manager and revolutionizing the way software products are conceived, built, and brought to market. We will examine the growing influence of artificial intelligence (AI) and machine learning (ML) in product development, from automating routine tasks to generating data-driven insights that inform product decisions. We will also discuss the rising importance of data-driven product management, where every decision is backed by rigorous analysis and experimentation.

Furthermore, we will explore the shift towards customer-centric product development, where user feedback and data are central to every stage of the product lifecycle. We will also touch upon the ethical considerations that are becoming increasingly important in product management, as software products become more pervasive and impactful in our lives.

In this chapter, you will:

- **Discover the potential of AI and ML in product management:** Learn how these technologies can automate tasks, generate insights, and personalize user experiences.
- **Embrace data-driven decision-making:** Explore how to leverage data analytics and experimentation to optimize product performance and drive growth.
- **Adopt a customer-centric approach:** Understand the importance of placing the user at the center of your product development process.
- **Navigate ethical considerations:** Grasp the ethical implications of your product decisions and build products that are responsible and beneficial to society.

By staying abreast of these emerging trends and adapting your approach, you can position yourself at the forefront of innovation, create products that truly resonate with users, and ensure the long-term success of your product management career. This chapter will provide you with the insights and knowledge needed to navigate the ever-changing landscape of software product management and embrace the future with confidence.

8.1 Artificial Intelligence and Machine Learning: The Rise of Intelligent Product Management

Artificial Intelligence (AI) and Machine Learning (ML) are no longer confined to the realms of science fiction. They are rapidly transforming industries across the board, and software product management is no exception. From automating mundane tasks to generating powerful insights, AI and ML are revolutionizing the way product managers operate, enabling them to make data-driven decisions, personalize user experiences, and drive innovation at an unprecedented pace.

AI and ML in Product Management: A Game-Changer

The integration of AI and ML into product management is ushering in a new era of intelligent product management, where machines augment human capabilities and empower product teams to achieve new levels of efficiency and effectiveness.

Here are some key ways AI and ML are transforming product management:

1. **Automating Routine Tasks:** AI-powered tools can automate repetitive and time-consuming tasks such as data entry, report generation, and customer support inquiries. This frees up product managers to focus on more strategic and creative aspects of their role.
2. **Generating Data-Driven Insights:** ML algorithms can analyze vast amounts of user data to uncover hidden patterns, trends, and correlations. This information can be used to identify user preferences, predict behavior, and personalize product experiences.
3. **Personalizing User Experiences:** AI-powered recommendation engines, chatbots, and virtual assistants can deliver personalized experiences to users, increasing engagement, satisfaction, and conversion rates.
4. **Predicting User Churn:** ML models can analyze user behavior data to predict which users are likely to churn, allowing product managers to intervene with targeted retention strategies.

5. **Optimizing Pricing and Promotions:** AI algorithms can analyze market data, competitor pricing, and customer behavior to optimize pricing strategies and promotional offers.
6. **Enhancing Product Discovery:** AI-powered tools can analyze customer feedback, online reviews, and social media conversations to identify emerging needs and trends, helping product managers discover new product ideas and opportunities.
7. **Streamlining Product Development:** AI can assist in various stages of the product development process, from generating design concepts to automating code reviews and testing.

Challenges and Considerations:

While the potential of AI and ML in product management is vast, there are also challenges and considerations to be aware of:

- **Data Quality and Bias:** AI and ML models are only as good as the data they are trained on. Ensuring data quality and mitigating biases are critical for accurate and fair outcomes.
- **Ethical Implications:** The use of AI in product management raises ethical questions around privacy, transparency, and accountability. Product managers need to consider the ethical implications of their decisions and ensure that AI is used responsibly.
- **Skills and Expertise:** Implementing and leveraging AI and ML effectively requires a certain level of technical expertise. Product managers may need to upskill or collaborate with data scientists and engineers to get the most out of these technologies.

The Future of AI and ML in Product Management:

The integration of AI and ML into product management is still in its early stages, but the potential for transformation is immense. As these technologies continue to evolve and mature, we can expect to see even more innovative applications that will further empower product managers and revolutionize the way software products are built and delivered.

By embracing AI and ML, product managers can gain a competitive edge, deliver more personalized and engaging experiences to users, and drive innovation in ways that were previously unimaginable. The rise of intelligent product management is not just a trend; it's a fundamental shift that will shape the future of the software industry.

8.2 Data-Driven Product Management: The Power of Informed Decisions

Data-driven product management is an approach that leverages data and analytics to inform every stage of the product lifecycle, from ideation and development to launch and optimization. It involves using quantitative and qualitative data to validate assumptions, measure progress, identify opportunities, and make informed decisions that drive product success.

The Importance of Data-Driven Product Management

In today's data-rich environment, relying solely on intuition or gut feeling is no longer sufficient. Data-driven product management enables you to:

- **Validate Assumptions:** Test hypotheses about user behavior, product features, and market trends to ensure that your decisions are based on evidence rather than guesswork.

- **Measure Progress:** Track key performance indicators (KPIs) to monitor the progress of your product and initiatives, identify bottlenecks, and measure the impact of your efforts.
- **Identify Opportunities:** Uncover hidden patterns and trends in your data that reveal untapped opportunities for growth and innovation.
- **Make Informed Decisions:** Use data-driven insights to make better decisions about product features, pricing, marketing, and overall strategy.
- **Optimize the User Experience:** Understand how users interact with your product and identify areas where the user experience can be improved.
- **Increase Efficiency:** Streamline processes, allocate resources effectively, and eliminate waste by basing decisions on data-driven insights.
- **Drive Innovation:** Identify emerging trends and customer needs to fuel innovation and create products that meet the evolving demands of the market.

Data Sources for Product Management:

Product managers can draw from a variety of data sources to inform their decisions:

- **Product Analytics:** Data on user behavior, engagement, and conversion within the product.
- **Marketing Analytics:** Data on marketing campaign performance, website traffic, and lead generation.
- **Sales Data:** Data on sales volume, revenue, and customer acquisition costs.
- **Customer Feedback:** Data from surveys, interviews, focus groups, and social media.

- **Market Research:** Data on market trends, competitor analysis, and industry reports.
- **A/B Testing:** Data from experiments that compare different versions of the product or marketing campaigns.

The Data-Driven Product Management Process:

1. **Define Goals and KPIs:** Clearly articulate the goals you want to achieve with your product and identify the key metrics that will measure your progress.
2. **Collect and Analyze Data:** Use analytics tools and techniques to collect relevant data and analyze it to identify trends, patterns, and insights.
3. **Develop Hypotheses:** Formulate hypotheses based on your data analysis and test them through experimentation or further data collection.
4. **Make Decisions:** Use the insights gained from your data analysis to make informed decisions about product features, pricing, marketing, and overall strategy.
5. **Measure and Iterate:** Track the impact of your decisions and iterate as needed based on the data you collect.

Building a Data-Driven Culture:

Creating a data-driven culture within your organization requires:

- **Leadership Support:** Executives and managers need to champion data-driven decision-making and set an example for the rest of the organization.

- **Access to Data:** Ensure that all relevant stakeholders have access to the data they need to make informed decisions.
- **Data Literacy:** Provide training and resources to help employees understand how to interpret and use data effectively.
- **Experimentation Mindset:** Encourage experimentation and a willingness to learn from failures.
- **Continuous Improvement:** Establish a process for regularly reviewing and acting on data-driven insights.

By embracing a data-driven approach, product managers can transform the way they work, making more informed decisions, driving innovation, and creating products that truly resonate with their target audience. Data-driven product management is not just a trend; it's a fundamental shift that is reshaping the product management landscape and empowering organizations to achieve greater success in the digital age.

8.3 Customer-Centric Product Development: Building Products That Delight

In the modern software landscape, where user expectations are constantly evolving and competition is fierce, a customer-centric approach to product development has become essential for long-term success. Customer-centric product development (CCPD) is a philosophy that places the user at the heart of every decision, from ideation to launch and beyond. It's about deeply understanding your users' needs, preferences, and behaviors, and using that knowledge to create products that truly resonate with them.

The Principles of Customer-Centric Product Development:

1. **Empathy:** Put yourself in the shoes of your users. Understand their goals, motivations, and pain points.
2. **Collaboration:** Involve users throughout the product development process, from ideation to testing and feedback.
3. **Data-Driven Insights:** Leverage data and analytics to gain insights into user behavior and preferences.
4. **Continuous Feedback:** Create a feedback loop to continuously gather and act on user feedback.
5. **Iterative Improvement:** Embrace an iterative approach to product development, continuously refining and improving the product based on user feedback and data.
6. **Personalization:** Tailor the product experience to the individual needs and preferences of users.
7. **Focus on Value:** Deliver value to users at every touchpoint, from the initial onboarding experience to ongoing customer support.

Benefits of Customer-Centric Product Development:

- **Increased Customer Satisfaction:** Products that are designed with the user in mind are more likely to meet their needs and expectations, leading to higher satisfaction and loyalty.
- **Improved Product-Market Fit:** By involving users in the development process, you can ensure that your product addresses real problems and offers genuine value.
- **Stronger Brand Reputation:** A commitment to customer-centricity can help you build a strong

brand reputation for listening to your customers and caring about their needs.

- **Increased Revenue:** Satisfied customers are more likely to recommend your product to others, leading to increased word-of-mouth marketing and higher revenue.
- **Competitive Advantage:** In a crowded market, a customer-centric approach can differentiate your product from the competition and give you a sustainable edge.

Implementing Customer-Centric Product Development:

1. **Conduct User Research:** Use a variety of methods, such as surveys, interviews, focus groups, and usability testing, to gather insights into user needs, behaviors, and preferences.
2. **Create User Personas:** Develop detailed profiles of your ideal customers, including their demographics, psychographics, goals, and pain points.
3. **Involve Users in the Design Process:** Seek feedback from users throughout the design process, from ideation to prototyping and testing.
4. **Collect and Analyze Feedback:** Create a system for collecting and analyzing user feedback, such as through surveys, feedback forms, or social media monitoring.
5. **Iterate and Improve:** Use feedback and data to continuously refine and improve your product.
6. **Personalize the Experience:** Tailor the product experience to the individual needs and preferences of users, using techniques such as recommendation engines or personalized content.
7. **Measure Customer Satisfaction:** Track customer satisfaction metrics, such as Net Promoter Score (NPS) and Customer Satisfaction Score (CSAT), to

gauge the effectiveness of your customer-centric approach.

By adopting a customer-centric approach to product development, you can create products that not only meet the needs of your target audience but also exceed their expectations. This can lead to increased customer loyalty, higher revenue, and a stronger competitive position in the market.

Additional Tips for Customer-Centric Product Development:

- **Focus on the Entire Customer Journey:** Consider the entire customer journey, from initial awareness to post-purchase support, and ensure that every touchpoint is designed with the user in mind.
- **Empower Your Team:** Give your team the autonomy and resources they need to make customer-centric decisions.
- **Celebrate Successes:** Recognize and reward team members who go above and beyond to deliver exceptional customer experiences.

Customer-centric product development is not just a buzzword; it's a philosophy that can transform the way you build products and drive lasting success in today's competitive market.

8.4 Ethical Considerations in Product Management: Building Responsible Products for a Better World

As software products become increasingly intertwined with our daily lives, the ethical implications of product decisions have never been more significant. Product managers hold a unique position of influence, shaping the design, functionality, and impact of products that can have far-reaching consequences for individuals, communities, and society as a whole. In this subchapter, we will explore the ethical considerations that product managers must grapple with, emphasizing the importance of building responsible products that prioritize user well-being, fairness, transparency, and societal benefit.

Key Ethical Considerations:

1. **Privacy and Data Protection:** With the vast amounts of data collected and processed by software products, protecting user privacy is of paramount importance. Product managers must ensure that data collection practices are transparent, that user data is secure, and that users have control over how their data is used.

2. **Bias and Discrimination:** Algorithms and machine learning models can inadvertently perpetuate biases and discrimination if not carefully designed and monitored. Product managers must be vigilant in identifying and mitigating bias in their products, ensuring that they are fair and equitable for all users.

3. **Transparency and Explainability:** Users have a right to understand how decisions are made that affect them. Product managers should strive for transparency in their algorithms and decision-making processes, providing explanations when requested and ensuring that users are not unfairly disadvantaged.

4. **Accessibility:** Software products should be designed to be accessible to all users, including those with disabilities. Product managers should

consider accessibility from the outset, incorporating inclusive design principles and adhering to accessibility guidelines.

5. **Addiction and Mental Health:** Some software products, particularly social media and gaming platforms, can be designed in ways that promote addictive behaviors or negatively impact mental health. Product managers should be mindful of these potential harms and strive to design products that promote healthy usage patterns.

6. **Environmental Impact:** The production and use of software products can have a significant environmental impact. Product managers should consider the environmental consequences of their decisions, from the energy consumption of data centers to the disposal of electronic waste.

7. **Social Impact:** Software products can have a profound impact on society, both positive and negative. Product managers should consider the broader societal implications of their products, striving to create products that contribute to the greater good.

Strategies for Ethical Product Management:

- **Embed Ethics into the Product Development Process:** Integrate ethical considerations into every stage of the product lifecycle, from ideation to launch and beyond.

- **Conduct Ethical Impact Assessments:** Assess the potential ethical risks and benefits of your product and develop strategies to mitigate risks and maximize benefits.

- **Establish Ethical Guidelines and Principles:** Develop a set of ethical guidelines and principles that guide your product decisions and actions.

- **Engage with Diverse Stakeholders:** Seek input from a diverse range of stakeholders, including users, ethicists, regulators, and community groups.
- **Monitor and Evaluate:** Continuously monitor the impact of your product on users and society, and make adjustments as needed.

By embracing ethical considerations, product managers can build products that not only meet market demands but also contribute to a better world. Ethical product management is not just a moral imperative; it's a strategic advantage that can enhance brand reputation, foster trust with users, and drive long-term success.

Emerging Trends in Software Product Management Action List

1. **Embrace Artificial Intelligence (AI) and Machine Learning (ML):**
   - Identify tasks that can be automated: Look for repetitive or time-consuming tasks that can be handled by AI-powered tools.
   - Leverage data-driven insights: Use ML algorithms to analyze user data and generate insights that can inform product decisions.
   - Personalize user experiences: Implement AI-powered recommendation engines, chatbots, or virtual assistants to tailor the product experience to individual users.
   - Predict user churn: Utilize ML models to identify users who are at risk of churning and implement proactive retention strategies.
   - Optimize pricing and promotions: Employ AI algorithms to analyze market data and

customer behavior to optimize pricing and promotional campaigns.

2. **Adopt a Data-Driven Product Management Approach:**
    - Define clear goals and KPIs: Establish measurable objectives and identify the metrics that will track your progress.
    - Collect and analyze data: Use analytics tools to gather data from various sources and analyze it to uncover trends and insights.
    - Develop hypotheses and test them: Use data to validate assumptions and experiment with different approaches.
    - Make informed decisions: Base your product decisions on data-driven insights, not just intuition or gut feeling.
    - Measure and iterate: Continuously track the impact of your decisions and make adjustments as needed.

3. **Implement Customer-Centric Product Development:**
    - Conduct user research: Gather insights into user needs, behaviors, and preferences through surveys, interviews, focus groups, and usability testing.
    - Create user personas: Develop detailed profiles of your ideal customers to guide your product decisions.
    - Involve users in the design process: Seek feedback from users throughout the development process, from ideation to testing and launch.
    - Collect and analyze feedback: Create a feedback loop to continuously gather and act on user feedback.

- o Iterate and improve: Use feedback and data to refine and enhance your product continuously.
- o Personalize the experience: Tailor the product experience to the individual needs and preferences of users.

4. **Prioritize Ethical Considerations:**
   - o Embed ethics into the development process: Integrate ethical considerations into every stage of the product lifecycle.
   - o Conduct ethical impact assessments: Assess the potential ethical risks and benefits of your product and develop strategies to mitigate risks.
   - o Establish ethical guidelines: Create a set of ethical principles that guide your product decisions and actions.
   - o Engage with diverse stakeholders: Seek input from a variety of perspectives, including users, ethicists, regulators, and community groups.
   - o Monitor and evaluate: Continuously monitor the impact of your product on users and society, and make adjustments as needed.

By incorporating these actions into your product management practice, you can embrace emerging trends, harness the power of data and AI, prioritize user needs, and build responsible products that make a positive impact on the world.

Chapter 9: Building and Leading Product Teams: Cultivating Collaboration and Innovation

A software product is not built in isolation. It is the result of a collaborative effort by a diverse team of talented individuals, each bringing their unique skills, perspectives, and expertise to the table. As a product manager, your ability to build and lead a high-performing product team is crucial to the success of your product. This chapter delves into the art and science of assembling, nurturing, and empowering a team that can drive innovation, overcome challenges, and deliver exceptional results.

We will explore the essential elements of building a cohesive product team, from identifying the right talent and fostering a culture of collaboration to setting clear goals and providing effective leadership. We will discuss the importance of diversity and inclusion in building a team that can approach problems from multiple angles and generate creative solutions. We will also delve into the challenges of managing cross-functional teams, where individuals from different disciplines must work together seamlessly to achieve a common goal.

In this chapter, you will:

- **Learn how to identify and hire top product talent:** Discover strategies for attracting, interviewing, and selecting the right individuals to build a high-performing team.
- **Cultivate a culture of collaboration and innovation:** Foster an environment where team members feel empowered to share ideas, challenge assumptions, and take calculated risks.

- **Set clear goals and expectations:** Establish a shared vision and roadmap for the team, define individual roles and responsibilities, and provide clear expectations for performance.
- **Provide effective leadership and mentorship:** Guide, support, and empower your team members to reach their full potential.
- **Manage cross-functional collaboration:** Navigate the complexities of working with individuals from different disciplines, ensuring effective communication and coordination.

By mastering the art of building and leading product teams, you can unlock the collective potential of your team members, foster a culture of innovation, and deliver exceptional products that delight users and drive business success. This chapter will provide you with the tools, insights, and strategies to become a true leader of product teams, inspiring and empowering your team to achieve greatness.

9.1 Hiring and Developing Product Talent: Building a High-Performing Team

A product manager is only as good as the team they build. Assembling a team of skilled, passionate, and collaborative individuals is essential for driving innovation, overcoming challenges, and achieving product success. This subchapter will explore the art and science of hiring and developing product talent, equipping you with the strategies and tools to attract, nurture, and retain the best minds in the field.

Identifying Top Product Talent: What to Look For

The ideal product manager possesses a unique blend of skills and qualities that enable them to thrive in this multifaceted role. When evaluating candidates, look for the following key traits:

- **Customer Obsession:** A deep understanding of customer needs and a relentless focus on delivering value to users.
- **Strategic Thinking:** The ability to think strategically, analyze market trends, and develop a compelling product vision.
- **Data-Driven Decision-Making:** The ability to gather, analyze, and interpret data to inform product decisions.
- **Communication and Collaboration:** Strong communication skills and the ability to collaborate effectively with cross-functional teams.
- **Technical Acumen:** A solid understanding of technology and how it can be leveraged to solve problems and create value.
- **Problem-Solving Skills:** The ability to identify and solve complex problems creatively and effectively.
- **Leadership and Influence:** The ability to inspire and motivate teams, build consensus, and drive results.
- **Adaptability and Resilience:** The ability to thrive in a fast-paced and ever-changing environment.

Hiring Strategies for Product Managers:

1. **Clearly Define the Role:** Create a detailed job description that outlines the responsibilities, qualifications, and expectations for the role.
2. **Leverage Your Network:** Tap into your professional network to source referrals and recommendations for potential candidates.

3. **Utilize Online Job Boards:** Post your job openings on relevant online job boards, such as LinkedIn, Indeed, or Glassdoor.
4. **Attend Industry Events:** Network with potential candidates at industry conferences, meetups, and events.
5. **Conduct Thorough Interviews:** Develop a structured interview process that includes behavioral, situational, and technical questions to assess the candidate's skills and experience.
6. **Assess Cultural Fit:** Ensure that the candidate's values and work style align with your company culture.

Developing Product Talent: Nurturing Growth and Potential

Once you have hired talented individuals, it's important to invest in their development to ensure their continued growth and success. Here are some strategies for developing product talent:

1. **Mentorship and Coaching:** Pair new product managers with experienced mentors who can provide guidance, support, and feedback.
2. **Training and Development Programs:** Offer training programs on relevant topics, such as product management methodologies, data analysis, and leadership skills.
3. **Opportunities for Growth:** Provide opportunities for product managers to take on new challenges and responsibilities, such as leading a new product initiative or managing a larger team.
4. **Regular Feedback:** Provide regular feedback on performance, both positive and constructive, to help product managers identify areas for improvement.

5. **Create a Learning Culture:** Encourage a culture of continuous learning and development, where team members are encouraged to share knowledge and learn from each other.

By investing in the development of your product team, you can create a high-performing team that is equipped to tackle any challenge, drive innovation, and deliver exceptional results. A strong product team is the foundation for building successful products that meet the needs of your customers and propel your business forward.

9.2 Fostering a Culture of Innovation: Unleashing the Power of Creativity

A high-performing product team is not just a collection of skilled individuals; it is a collective of creative minds working together towards a common goal. Fostering a culture of innovation is essential for cultivating a team that can generate groundbreaking ideas, challenge assumptions, and drive the product forward. This subchapter will explore the key principles and practices that can help you create an environment where innovation thrives.

Key Elements of an Innovation Culture:

1. Psychological Safety:

A culture of innovation starts with psychological safety – the belief that one can speak up without fear of reprisal or humiliation. When team members feel safe to express their ideas, challenge the status quo, and even make mistakes, they are more likely to take risks, experiment, and ultimately innovate.

2. Open Communication and Collaboration:

Encourage open and transparent communication within your team. Create channels for sharing ideas, providing feedback, and collaborating on projects. Break down silos and foster cross-functional collaboration to encourage diverse perspectives and generate new ideas.

3. Empowerment and Autonomy:

Give your team members the autonomy to make decisions and take ownership of their work. Encourage them to experiment, try new things, and learn from their mistakes. When people feel empowered, they are more likely to be creative and take initiative.

4. Tolerance for Failure:

Innovation often involves taking risks, and not all experiments will succeed. It's important to create a culture where failure is viewed as a learning opportunity rather than a cause for blame. Encourage your team to embrace failure, learn from their mistakes, and move forward with renewed determination.

5. Recognition and Rewards:

Recognize and reward innovative ideas and efforts, even if they don't always lead to immediate success. Celebrate small wins and milestones, and create a culture where creativity and risk-taking are valued.

6. Continuous Learning and Development:

Encourage your team members to continuously learn and develop their skills. Provide opportunities for training, workshops, conferences, and access to resources that can help them stay ahead of the curve. A culture of continuous learning fosters curiosity, exploration, and a thirst for knowledge – all essential ingredients for innovation.

7. Leadership Support:

Innovation cannot thrive without strong leadership support. Leaders must set the tone for an innovation culture by modeling the desired behaviors, empowering their teams, and providing the resources and support needed to bring new ideas to fruition.

Practical Tips for Fostering Innovation:

- Hold regular brainstorming sessions and idea jams.
- Encourage experimentation and prototyping.
- Create a "failure wall" where team members can share their learnings from unsuccessful experiments.
- Establish an innovation fund to support promising ideas.
- Celebrate innovation successes and share them with the wider organization.
- Provide opportunities for team members to attend industry events and conferences.
- Encourage cross-functional collaboration and knowledge sharing.

By implementing these principles and practices, you can create a vibrant and dynamic innovation culture within your product team. A culture where creativity flourishes, ideas are encouraged, and the pursuit of excellence is a shared passion. Such a culture will not only lead to groundbreaking product innovations but also foster a sense of purpose, engagement, and fulfillment among your team members.

9.3 Managing Cross-Functional Teams: Harmonizing Diverse Skills for Product Success

In the complex landscape of software product development, achieving success often hinges on the seamless collaboration of individuals from diverse disciplines. Cross-functional teams, comprised of members from engineering, design, marketing, sales, and other departments, bring together a wealth of knowledge and perspectives to tackle the multifaceted challenges of creating and launching a product. However, managing such teams effectively requires a unique set of skills and strategies to foster collaboration, alignment, and shared purpose.

The Dynamics of Cross-Functional Teams:

Cross-functional teams are characterized by their diversity in terms of skills, backgrounds, and perspectives. This diversity can be a source of immense strength, fueling creativity, innovation, and problem-solving. However, it can also lead to challenges such as miscommunication, conflicting priorities, and differing work styles.

Common challenges faced by cross-functional teams:

- **Communication Barriers:** Team members may use different jargon, have different communication styles, or lack a shared understanding of the product vision.
- **Conflicting Priorities:** Different departments may have competing priorities and goals, leading to

conflicts over resource allocation and decision-making.

- **Differing Work Styles:** Individuals from different disciplines may have different approaches to work, leading to misunderstandings and inefficiencies.
- **Lack of Trust:** Building trust and rapport across different departments can be challenging, especially when team members are not used to working together.

Strategies for Effective Cross-Functional Team Management:

1. **Establish a Clear Vision and Shared Goals:** Ensure that all team members have a clear understanding of the product vision, strategic goals, and their individual roles and responsibilities. This will help to create a sense of shared purpose and alignment.
2. **Foster Open Communication and Collaboration:** Encourage open and transparent communication between team members. Create channels for sharing ideas, providing feedback, and resolving conflicts constructively.
3. **Build Trust and Rapport:** Encourage team members to get to know each other on a personal level. Organize team-building activities, social events, or informal gatherings to foster trust and camaraderie.
4. **Embrace Diversity:** Recognize and celebrate the diversity of skills, backgrounds, and perspectives within your team. Leverage this diversity to generate creative solutions and innovative ideas.
5. **Establish Clear Decision-Making Processes:** Define clear decision-making processes and empower team members to make decisions within

their areas of expertise. This will help to avoid bottlenecks and ensure that decisions are made quickly and efficiently.

6. **Provide Resources and Support:** Ensure that your team has the resources and support they need to succeed, including access to training, tools, and technology.

7. **Celebrate Successes:** Recognize and celebrate the achievements of the team, both big and small. This will help to boost morale and foster a sense of shared accomplishment.

The Product Manager's Role in Leading Cross-Functional Teams:

The product manager plays a crucial role in leading and managing cross-functional teams. They are the glue that holds the team together, ensuring that everyone is working towards a common goal. Product managers must be skilled communicators, facilitators, and diplomats, able to navigate complex interpersonal dynamics and foster a collaborative environment.

By implementing these strategies and embracing the diversity of cross-functional teams, product managers can unlock the full potential of their teams, drive innovation, and create products that truly meet the needs of their users.

Building and Leading Product Teams Action List

1. **Hiring and Developing Product Talent:**
   o Define the ideal product manager profile: Outline the essential skills, qualities, and experience you seek in candidates.

- Leverage your network: Tap into your professional contacts for referrals and recommendations.
- Utilize online job boards and platforms: Post job openings on LinkedIn, Indeed, Glassdoor, and other relevant platforms.
- Attend industry events: Network with potential candidates at conferences, meetups, and workshops.
- Conduct thorough interviews: Design a structured interview process to assess candidates' skills, experience, and cultural fit.
- Invest in ongoing development: Provide mentorship, training, feedback, and growth opportunities for your team members.

2. **Fostering a Culture of Innovation:**
   - Create psychological safety: Encourage open communication and create a safe space for sharing ideas and taking risks.
   - Promote collaboration: Facilitate open communication channels, cross-functional collaboration, and knowledge sharing.
   - Empower and provide autonomy: Trust your team members to make decisions and take ownership of their work.
   - Embrace failure as a learning opportunity: Encourage experimentation and view setbacks as a chance to learn and grow.
   - Recognize and reward innovation: Celebrate successes and acknowledge contributions, even small ones.
   - Invest in continuous learning: Provide resources for ongoing learning and development to foster curiosity and growth.

- o Lead by example: Demonstrate the behaviors and values you want to see in your team.
3. **Managing Cross-Functional Teams:**
    - o Establish a clear vision and shared goals: Ensure everyone understands the product vision, strategic goals, and their individual roles and responsibilities.
    - o Foster open communication and collaboration: Encourage transparent communication, regular feedback, and constructive conflict resolution.
    - o Build trust and rapport: Organize team-building activities and create opportunities for personal connection.
    - o Embrace diversity: Recognize and value the unique perspectives and strengths that each team member brings.
    - o Establish clear decision-making processes: Define how decisions will be made and empower team members to take ownership.
    - o Provide resources and support: Ensure your team has access to the tools, training, and information they need to succeed.
    - o Celebrate successes: Acknowledge and reward team accomplishments to boost morale and maintain momentum.

By implementing this action list, you can create a high-performing product team that thrives on collaboration, embraces innovation, and consistently delivers exceptional results.

Part IV: Additional Topics

Chapter 10: Product Management Tools and Technologies: Empowering Your Workflow

In the fast-paced and data-driven world of software product management, having the right tools and technologies at your disposal can make all the difference. From streamlining communication and collaboration to analyzing user data and prioritizing features, these tools empower product managers to work more efficiently, make informed decisions, and ultimately deliver exceptional products that meet the needs of their users.

This chapter will delve into the diverse landscape of product management tools and technologies, exploring the various categories of tools available and highlighting their benefits and use cases. We will discuss the essential tools for road mapping and prioritization, collaboration and communication, user feedback and analytics, prototyping and design, and project management and task tracking.

Whether you're a seasoned product manager looking to optimize your workflow or a newcomer seeking to build your toolkit, this chapter will provide a comprehensive overview of the essential tools and technologies that can help you streamline your processes, enhance collaboration, and drive product success.

In this chapter, you will:

- **Discover a wide range of product management tools:** Explore the various categories of tools available to support different aspects of the product management process.

- **Understand the benefits of each tool:** Learn how specific tools can help you streamline communication, prioritize features, analyze data, and manage projects more effectively.
- **Choose the right tools for your needs:** Identify the tools that best align with your team's size, budget, and specific requirements.
- **Learn how to implement and use these tools effectively:** Get tips and best practices for integrating these tools into your workflow and maximizing their potential.

By leveraging the right tools and technologies, you can empower your team, streamline your processes, and elevate your product management practice to new heights. This chapter will guide you through the ever-evolving landscape of product management tools, helping you select and implement the solutions that will best support your journey towards creating exceptional products that delight your users.

10.1 Roadmapping and Prioritization Tools: Crafting Your Product's Journey

Roadmapping and prioritization tools are essential for product managers to visualize the product's trajectory, communicate the strategy to stakeholders, and make informed decisions about which features to prioritize. These tools help product managers to create a shared understanding of the product vision and roadmap, track progress, and adapt to changing market conditions.

Benefits of Roadmapping and Prioritization Tools:

- **Visualize the Product's Evolution:** Create a visual representation of the product roadmap, outlining key milestones, features, and timelines.
- **Communicate the Strategy:** Share the roadmap with stakeholders to ensure alignment and manage expectations.
- **Prioritize Features:** Use prioritization frameworks (e.g., MoSCoW, RICE, Kano Model) to determine which features to build first based on their impact on customer value and business goals.
- **Track Progress:** Monitor the progress of features and releases to ensure the product stays on track.
- **Adapt to Change:** Easily update the roadmap to reflect changing priorities, market conditions, or customer feedback.

Popular Roadmapping and Prioritization Tools:

- **ProductPlan:** This intuitive platform offers a user-friendly interface for creating and sharing visual roadmaps. It allows for easy collaboration, customization, and integration with other tools like Jira and Trello.
- **Aha!:** This comprehensive product management platform includes robust roadmapping features, along with tools for idea management, feedback collection, and progress tracking. It's suitable for both small and large teams.
- **Roadmunk:** This flexible tool allows you to create multiple roadmaps for different audiences and purposes. It offers integrations with popular project management tools and provides powerful data visualization capabilities.
- **ProdPad:** This collaborative platform focuses on capturing and prioritizing product ideas, creating lean roadmaps, and gathering customer feedback.

It's designed for agile teams who value flexibility and iteration.

- **Productboard:** This end-to-end product management solution offers features for road-mapping, prioritization, feedback collection, and user research. It's a comprehensive platform suitable for larger organizations with complex product portfolios.

Choosing the Right Tool:

The best road-mapping and prioritization tool for your team will depend on various factors, including:

- **Team Size:** Some tools are better suited for small teams, while others are designed for larger organizations with complex product portfolios.
- **Budget:** Consider the pricing and licensing options of different tools to find one that fits your budget.
- **Features:** Evaluate the features offered by each tool to see if they align with your specific needs.
- **Integration:** If you use other product management or development tools, choose a roadmapping tool that integrates with them seamlessly.
- **Usability:** The tool should be easy to use and intuitive for your team members to adopt.

Tips for Using Roadmapping and Prioritization Tools:

- **Start with a clear vision:** Before you start building your roadmap, ensure you have a clear understanding of your product vision and strategic goals.
- **Involve stakeholders:** Gather input from key stakeholders, including customers, executives, and

team members, to ensure that the roadmap reflects their needs and priorities.

- **Focus on outcomes, not outputs:** Prioritize features based on the value they deliver to customers and the business, not just the number of features you can build.
- **Keep it high-level:** Don't get bogged down in too much detail. The roadmap should provide a clear overview of the product's direction, not a detailed specification.
- **Be flexible:** The roadmap is not set in stone. It should be a living document that evolves as the product and market landscape change.
- **Communicate regularly:** Share the roadmap with stakeholders regularly and communicate any updates or changes in a timely manner.

By leveraging the right roadmapping and prioritization tools and following best practices, you can create a clear and compelling roadmap that guides your team towards success while remaining adaptable to change.

10.2 Collaboration and Communication Platforms: Fostering Seamless Teamwork

Effective communication and collaboration are the lifeblood of any successful product team. With the rise of remote work and distributed teams, the need for robust collaboration and communication platforms has become even more critical. These tools enable teams to stay connected, share information seamlessly, and work together efficiently, regardless of their physical location.

Benefits of Collaboration and Communication Platforms:

- **Streamlined Communication:** Centralize communication channels, eliminating the need to switch between multiple tools and platforms.
- **Enhanced Collaboration:** Facilitate real-time collaboration on documents, projects, and tasks, improving productivity and reducing bottlenecks.
- **Increased Transparency:** Provide a transparent view of project progress, tasks, and deadlines, ensuring everyone is on the same page.
- **Improved Decision-Making:** Enable quick and informed decision-making through real-time discussions and feedback.
- **Stronger Team Culture:** Foster a sense of community and camaraderie among team members, even when working remotely.

Key Features to Look for in Collaboration and Communication Platforms:

- **Messaging and Chat:** Real-time messaging, group chat, and direct messaging capabilities for quick and easy communication.
- **File Sharing and Storage:** Securely share and store documents, images, and other files in a central location.
- **Video Conferencing and Screen Sharing:** Conduct virtual meetings and presentations, share screens, and collaborate in real-time.
- **Project Management and Task Tracking:** Create and assign tasks, track progress, and manage deadlines.
- **Integration with Other Tools:** Seamlessly integrate with other tools in your product management stack, such as roadmapping, design, and development tools.

- **Customization and Flexibility:** Adapt the platform to your team's specific needs and workflow.

Popular Collaboration and Communication Platforms:

- **Slack:** A popular messaging platform that offers real-time communication, file sharing, and integrations with various tools.
- **Microsoft Teams:** A comprehensive collaboration platform that includes messaging, video conferencing, file sharing, and integration with Microsoft Office suite.
- **Zoom:** A widely used video conferencing platform that offers high-quality video and audio, screen sharing, and recording capabilities.
- **Notion:** An all-in-one workspace that combines notes, documents, wikis, and project management tools in a single platform.
- **Confluence:** A team collaboration platform designed for creating and sharing knowledge, documentation, and project information.

Choosing the Right Platform:

The ideal collaboration and communication platform for your team will depend on your specific needs and budget. Consider the following factors when making your decision:

- **Team Size:** Choose a platform that can scale to accommodate the size of your team and the volume of communication and collaboration.
- **Features:** Select a platform that offers the features and functionality that are most important to your team, such as messaging, file sharing, video conferencing, and project management.

- **Ease of Use:** The platform should be intuitive and easy for your team members to use, minimizing the learning curve and maximizing adoption.
- **Security:** Ensure that the platform offers robust security features to protect sensitive data and communication.
- **Cost:** Consider the pricing and licensing options of different platforms to find one that fits your budget.

By selecting the right collaboration and communication platform and implementing it effectively, you can empower your team to work together seamlessly, communicate effectively, and achieve their goals more efficiently.

10.3 User Feedback and Analytics Tools: Listening to the Voice of the Customer

In the realm of software product management, understanding your users is paramount. User feedback and analytics tools serve as a direct line of communication between you and your customers, providing invaluable insights into their needs, preferences, behaviors, and pain points. These tools empower product managers to make data-driven decisions, prioritize features, and ultimately create products that resonate with their target audience.

The Importance of User Feedback and Analytics:

- **Understanding User Needs:** Gathering feedback directly from users helps you identify their most pressing needs and pain points, ensuring your product solves real problems.
- **Validating Assumptions:** User feedback can validate or challenge your assumptions about what users want and how they use your product.

- **Measuring Satisfaction:** Tracking user satisfaction metrics helps you gauge how well your product is meeting user expectations and identify areas for improvement.
- **Identifying Trends:** Analyzing user behavior data can reveal patterns and trends that can inform your product roadmap and marketing strategies.
- **Prioritizing Features:** User feedback can help you prioritize features and enhancements that will deliver the most value to your customers.
- **Improving the User Experience:** Understanding how users interact with your product allows you to identify and address usability issues, ultimately enhancing the overall user experience.

Types of User Feedback and Analytics Tools:

1. **Feedback Collection Tools:**

- **Surveys and Polls:** Gather quantitative data on user opinions, preferences, and satisfaction.
- **Feedback Widgets and Forms:** Allow users to submit feedback directly from your website or app.
- **User Interviews and Focus Groups:** Conduct in-depth qualitative research to understand user motivations and pain points.
- **Social Media Monitoring:** Track mentions of your product on social media to gauge sentiment and gather feedback.

2. **Analytics Tools:**

- **Product Analytics:** Track user behavior within your product, such as feature usage, navigation patterns, and conversion funnels.

- **Web Analytics:** Analyze website traffic, visitor demographics, and user behavior on your website.
- **App Analytics:** Track app downloads, user engagement, and retention rates for mobile applications.

Popular User Feedback and Analytics Tools:

- **Hotjar:** Provides heatmaps, session recordings, and feedback polls to visualize user behavior and gather qualitative feedback.
- **UserTesting:** Allows you to test your product with real users and get video feedback on their experience.
- **Qualtrics:** Offers a comprehensive suite of tools for creating and distributing surveys, analyzing feedback, and managing customer experience programs.
- **Pendo:** A product experience platform that combines product analytics, user feedback, and in-app guides to help you understand and improve the user experience.
- **Amplitude:** A product intelligence platform that provides deep insights into user behavior and helps you optimize your product for growth.

Choosing the Right Tools:

The best user feedback and analytics tools for your team will depend on your specific needs and budget. Consider the following factors when making your decision:

- **Type of Data:** What kind of data do you want to collect? Do you need quantitative data, qualitative data, or both?

- **Ease of Use:** How easy is the tool to implement and use? Does it integrate with your existing workflow?
- **Features:** What features are most important to you? Do you need advanced segmentation, cohort analysis, or A/B testing capabilities?
- **Cost:** What is your budget for user feedback and analytics tools?

By leveraging the right tools and analyzing user feedback and data effectively, you can gain valuable insights into your users' needs and preferences, make informed product decisions, and ultimately create products that truly resonate with your target audience.

10.4 Prototyping and Design Tools: Bringing Ideas to Life

In the world of software product development, prototyping and design tools serve as the bridge between abstract concepts and tangible user experiences. They allow product managers, designers, and developers to visualize, experiment, and refine their ideas before investing significant time and resources in building the final product. These tools not only facilitate communication and collaboration but also enable teams to gather valuable feedback from users early in the development cycle, ensuring that the final product meets their needs and expectations.

Benefits of Prototyping and Design Tools:

- **Visualize Ideas:** Transform abstract concepts into interactive mockups and prototypes that can be easily understood and shared with stakeholders.
- **Test and Validate:** Gather feedback from users on early-stage designs to identify usability issues,

validate assumptions, and refine the product concept.

- **Iterate Quickly:** Rapidly create and iterate on different design options, allowing for faster experimentation and decision-making.
- **Improve Collaboration:** Facilitate communication and collaboration between designers, developers, and stakeholders by providing a shared visual language.
- **Reduce Risk and Cost:** Identify and address potential design flaws or usability issues early in the development process, saving time and resources in the long run.
- **Enhance User Experience:** Create user-centered designs that are intuitive, engaging, and enjoyable to use.

Types of Prototyping and Design Tools:

- **Low-Fidelity Prototyping Tools:** These tools allow you to quickly create basic mockups and wireframes to visualize the layout and structure of your product. They are ideal for early-stage ideation and concept testing. Examples include Balsamiq, MockFlow, and Whimsical.
- **High-Fidelity Prototyping Tools:** These tools offer more advanced features, such as interactive elements, animations, and transitions, allowing you to create realistic prototypes that closely resemble the final product. They are useful for user testing and gathering feedback on the overall user experience. Examples include Figma, InVision, and Axure RP.
- **UI Design Tools:** These tools focus on creating visually appealing user interfaces, offering features like design libraries, customizable components, and

collaboration tools. They are typically used by designers to create high-quality mockups and prototypes. Examples include Sketch, Adobe XD, and Framer.

Choosing the Right Tool:

The best prototyping and design tool for your team will depend on your specific needs and budget. Consider the following factors when making your decision:

- **Fidelity:** Do you need a tool for creating low-fidelity mockups, high-fidelity prototypes, or both?
- **Collaboration:** How important is real-time collaboration for your team? Does the tool offer features like commenting, version control, and shared workspaces?
- **Integration:** Does the tool integrate with other tools in your product management stack, such as project management or development tools?
- **Ease of Use:** Is the tool easy to learn and use, even for team members who are not designers?
- **Cost:** What is your budget for prototyping and design tools?

Tips for Using Prototyping and Design Tools:

- **Start Early:** Begin prototyping as soon as you have a basic idea of your product concept. This will help you validate your ideas and get feedback early in the development process.
- **Iterate Often:** Don't be afraid to experiment with different design options and iterate on your prototypes based on feedback.

- **Test with Real Users:** Get feedback from real users on your prototypes to identify usability issues and ensure that the design meets their needs.
- **Document Your Process:** Keep track of your design decisions and the feedback you receive to ensure that your team has a shared understanding of the product's evolution.

By incorporating prototyping and design tools into your product management workflow, you can create user-centered designs, streamline collaboration, and ultimately deliver products that delight your users.

10.5 Project Management and Task Tracking Tools: Staying Organized and on Schedule

The development of a software product involves a multitude of tasks, deadlines, dependencies, and team members. Without effective project management and task tracking tools, the process can quickly become chaotic, leading to missed deadlines, budget overruns, and ultimately, an unsatisfactory product. These tools provide a structured framework for organizing and tracking work, ensuring that everyone on the team knows what needs to be done, who is responsible for it, and when it needs to be completed.

Benefits of Project Management and Task Tracking Tools:

- **Improved Organization:** Centralize tasks, deadlines, and project information, eliminating the need for scattered spreadsheets and documents.
- **Enhanced Visibility:** Provide a clear overview of project progress, task status, and team workload,

allowing for better resource allocation and decision-making.

- **Increased Accountability:** Assign tasks to specific team members, track their progress, and ensure deadlines are met.
- **Streamlined Collaboration:** Facilitate collaboration by allowing team members to share updates, comments, and files within the tool.
- **Reduced Risk:** Identify potential bottlenecks or delays early on, allowing for proactive mitigation and risk management.
- **Data-Driven Insights:** Track key metrics like time spent on tasks, task completion rates, and project milestones to gain insights into team performance and identify areas for improvement.

Key Features to Look for in Project Management and Task Tracking Tools:

- **Task Management:** Create and assign tasks, set deadlines, and track progress.
- **Project Planning:** Create project plans, define milestones, and track dependencies.
- **Collaboration:** Enable team members to communicate and collaborate on tasks and projects.
- **Time Tracking:** Track time spent on tasks to measure productivity and identify bottlenecks.
- **Reporting and Analytics:** Generate reports on project progress, team performance, and other key metrics.
- **Integrations:** Seamlessly integrate with other tools in your product management stack, such as roadmapping, design, and communication tools.
- **Customization:** Adapt the tool to your team's specific workflow and preferences.

Popular Project Management and Task Tracking Tools:

- **Jira:** A widely used tool for agile project management, known for its powerful issue tracking and workflow customization capabilities.
- **Asana:** A flexible project management platform that offers various views, including lists, boards, and timelines, to cater to different work styles.
- **Trello:** A visual collaboration tool that uses Kanban boards to organize and track tasks. It's ideal for teams that prefer a simple and intuitive interface.
- **ClickUp:** A comprehensive project management platform that combines task management, document collaboration, time tracking, and reporting in a single tool.
- **Monday.com:** A customizable work operating system (Work OS) that allows teams to build their own workflows and automate processes.

Choosing the Right Tool:

The best project management and task tracking tool for your team will depend on your specific needs and budget. Consider the following factors when making your decision:

- **Team Size and Structure:** Choose a tool that can accommodate the size and complexity of your team.
- **Project Methodology:** Select a tool that aligns with your preferred project management methodology (e.g., Agile, Waterfall).
- **Features:** Prioritize the features that are most important to your team, such as task management, project planning, collaboration, time tracking, and reporting.
- **Ease of Use:** The tool should be intuitive and easy for your team members to use.

- **Integration:** Choose a tool that integrates with your other product management and development tools.
- **Cost:** Evaluate the pricing and licensing options of different tools to find one that fits your budget.

By selecting and implementing the right project management and task tracking tools, you can streamline your workflow, improve team communication and collaboration, and ensure that your projects are delivered on time and within budget.

Product Management Tools and Technologies Action List

1. **Roadmapping and Prioritization:**
   - Choose a roadmapping tool: Select a platform like ProductPlan, Aha!, Roadmunk, ProdPad, or Productboard based on your team's needs and budget.
   - Define your product vision and strategic goals: Ensure your roadmap aligns with your overall objectives.
   - Gather input from stakeholders: Include feedback from customers, executives, and team members to create a comprehensive roadmap.
   - Prioritize features based on value: Use prioritization frameworks like MoSCoW, RICE, or Kano to determine which features to build first.
   - Track progress and adapt: Regularly update your roadmap based on feedback, data, and changing market conditions.
2. **Collaboration and Communication:**
   - Select a collaboration platform: Choose a tool like Slack, Microsoft Teams, Zoom,

Notion, or Confluence based on your team's communication and collaboration needs.

- o Centralize communication: Use the platform for all team communication to avoid scattered conversations and information silos.
- o Encourage real-time collaboration: Leverage the platform's features for file sharing, video conferencing, and document collaboration.
- o Promote transparency: Keep everyone informed about project progress, tasks, and deadlines.
- o Foster a sense of community: Use the platform to build relationships, share ideas, and celebrate successes.

3. **User Feedback and Analytics:**
   - o Choose the right tools: Select feedback and analytics tools like Hotjar, UserTesting, Qualtrics, Pendo, or Amplitude based on the type of data you need and your budget.
   - o Gather user feedback: Use surveys, polls, feedback widgets, interviews, focus groups, and social media monitoring to collect both quantitative and qualitative feedback.
   - o Track user behavior: Implement analytics to monitor how users interact with your product, including feature usage, navigation patterns, and conversion funnels.
   - o Analyze and act on data: Identify trends, patterns, and areas for improvement to make data-driven product decisions.

4. **Prototyping and Design:**
   - o Select prototyping tools: Choose low-fidelity tools like Balsamiq, MockFlow, or Whimsical for early-stage ideation, and

high-fidelity tools like Figma, InVision, or Axure RP for realistic prototypes.
- o Create mockups and prototypes: Visualize your product concept and gather feedback from stakeholders and users.
- o Iterate and refine: Use feedback to improve your designs and ensure they meet user needs and expectations.
- o Test with real users: Conduct usability testing to identify and address any design flaws or usability issues.
5. **Project Management and Task Tracking:**
    - o Choose a project management tool: Select a tool like Jira, Asana, Trello, ClickUp, or Monday.com based on your team's size, project methodology, and desired features.
    - o Create a project plan: Outline tasks, deadlines, milestones, dependencies, and resource allocation.
    - o Assign tasks and track progress: Ensure every task has a clear owner and track its progress towards completion.
    - o Collaborate effectively: Use the tool to facilitate communication, share updates, and discuss challenges.
    - o Monitor key metrics: Track time spent on tasks, task completion rates, and project milestones to identify bottlenecks and optimize your workflow.

By incorporating these tools into your product management process, you can streamline your workflow, enhance collaboration, gather valuable user insights, and ultimately deliver successful software products that exceed customer expectations.

Chapter 11: Common Mistakes to Avoid in Product Management: Lessons Learned from the Trenches

The path of a software product manager is fraught with challenges and pitfalls. Even the most seasoned professionals can stumble, making missteps that can derail a product's development, launch, or long-term success. However, these mistakes are not inevitable. By learning from the experiences of others and understanding the common pitfalls that plague product management, you can proactively navigate these challenges and increase your chances of success.

This chapter will delve into the most prevalent mistakes that product managers make, drawing from real-world examples and case studies to illustrate their impact and consequences. We will examine the dangers of failing to define a clear vision and strategy, ignoring customer feedback, overpromising and underdelivering, micromanaging the team, neglecting data and analytics, resisting change, lacking communication and collaboration, focusing on features over benefits, and ignoring the competition.

For each mistake, we will provide practical advice and strategies for avoiding them, equipping you with the knowledge and tools to make informed decisions, build strong relationships with your team and stakeholders, and ultimately deliver exceptional products that meet the needs of your users and drive business growth.

Whether you're a seasoned product manager or just starting your journey, this chapter will serve as a valuable guide, helping you to avoid common pitfalls, learn from the mistakes of others, and chart a course towards product management excellence.

11.1 Failing to Define a Clear Vision and Strategy: A Recipe for Disaster

A ship without a rudder is at the mercy of the winds and currents. Similarly, a product without a clear vision and strategy is destined to drift aimlessly, wasting valuable time and resources. This common mistake in product management can manifest in various ways, from a vague and uninspiring vision statement to a lack of alignment between the product roadmap and the overall business goals.

The Consequences of a Lack of Vision and Strategy:

- **Misaligned Priorities:** When there's no clear vision, teams may focus on the wrong features, leading to products that don't resonate with users or address their needs effectively.
- **Wasted Resources:** Without a defined strategy, resources may be allocated inefficiently, resulting in missed opportunities and unnecessary expenditures.
- **Lack of Direction:** A team without a clear direction is like a ship without a compass. They may struggle to make decisions, prioritize tasks, and measure progress.
- **Demotivated Team:** When team members don't understand the purpose or impact of their work, their motivation and engagement can suffer, leading to lower productivity and higher turnover.
- **Missed Opportunities:** Without a strategic roadmap, you may miss out on emerging trends, competitive threats, or opportunities for growth.

How to Avoid This Mistake:

1. **Craft a Compelling Vision Statement:** Your vision statement should be a concise and inspiring declaration that articulates the long-term goal and desired impact of your product. It should be clear, memorable, and motivating.
2. **Develop a Comprehensive Product Strategy:** Your product strategy should be a well-defined plan that outlines how you will achieve your vision. It should include your target market, value proposition, key differentiators, go-to-market strategy, and roadmap.
3. **Communicate the Vision and Strategy Clearly:** Ensure that everyone on your team understands the vision and strategy and how their work contributes to achieving them. Share the vision and strategy regularly and invite feedback from your team.
4. **Align the Product Roadmap with Business Goals:** Make sure that the features and initiatives on your roadmap are aligned with the overall business goals and objectives. Regularly review and update your roadmap to ensure it remains relevant and aligned with your strategy.
5. **Use Data and Metrics to Measure Progress:** Track key performance indicators (KPIs) to measure your progress towards achieving your vision and strategic goals. Use data to identify areas where you are falling short and make necessary adjustments to your roadmap or strategy.

Case Study: The Importance of a Clear Vision

Consider the case of Kodak, a company that once dominated the photography industry. Despite inventing the digital camera, Kodak failed to adapt to the digital revolution because they lacked a clear vision for the future. They continued to focus on their traditional film business, missing out on the massive growth opportunities in digital photography. This failure to define a clear vision and strategy ultimately led to their decline.

By contrast, companies like Apple and Amazon have thrived because they have consistently articulated a clear vision and developed strategies to achieve it. Apple's vision of "making the best products in the world that enrich people's lives" has guided their product development and marketing efforts, resulting in a loyal customer base and a string of successful products.

A clear vision and strategy are not just nice-to-haves; they are essential for product management success. By taking the time to define your vision and develop a comprehensive strategy, you can set your product on a path towards achieving its full potential and delivering lasting value to your users.

11.2 Ignoring Customer Feedback and Needs: Building a Product in a Vacuum

Product managers are the bridge between the business and the customer. They are responsible for understanding the needs of the market and ensuring that the product they build addresses those needs effectively. Ignoring customer feedback and needs is akin to building a product in a vacuum, detached from the realities and preferences of the very people you are trying to serve.

The Perils of Ignoring Customer Feedback:

- **Irrelevant Products:** When you don't listen to your customers, you risk building products that don't solve real problems or address their pain points. This can lead to low adoption rates, poor user engagement, and ultimately, a failed product.

- **Missed Opportunities:** Customer feedback can be a goldmine of insights and ideas. Ignoring it means missing out on opportunities for innovation, improvement, and differentiation from the competition.
- **Damaged Reputation:** When customers feel unheard and their feedback ignored, it can lead to frustration and resentment, damaging your brand reputation and customer loyalty.
- **Increased Churn:** Users who feel that their needs are not being met are more likely to abandon your product and switch to a competitor who is more responsive to their feedback.
- **Wasted Resources:** Investing time and resources in developing features or products that customers don't want is a costly mistake that can drain your budget and delay your time to market.

How to Avoid This Mistake:

1. **Make Feedback a Priority:** Establish a culture where customer feedback is valued and actively sought. Create multiple channels for gathering feedback, such as surveys, feedback forms, user interviews, and social media monitoring.
2. **Listen Actively and Empathetically:** When you receive feedback, listen carefully and try to understand the underlying needs and motivations behind it. Respond to feedback promptly and acknowledge the customer's concerns.
3. **Involve Customers in the Development Process:** Invite customers to participate in beta testing, user

research, and focus groups. This will give you valuable insights into their needs and preferences.

4. **Analyze and Act on Feedback:** Regularly analyze customer feedback and use the insights to inform your product roadmap and decision-making. Prioritize features and improvements that address the most pressing customer needs.

5. **Close the Feedback Loop:** Communicate back to customers how their feedback has been incorporated into the product. This demonstrates that you value their input and are committed to building a product that meets their needs.

Case Study: The Importance of Listening to Customers

The story of Slack is a powerful example of how listening to customer feedback can lead to product success. In its early days, Slack was initially designed as an internal communication tool for a gaming company. However, the founders noticed that employees were using it for much more than just work communication. They were using it to collaborate on projects, share ideas, and build community.

By listening to this feedback and observing how users were actually using the product, the Slack team realized they had stumbled upon a much larger opportunity. They pivoted their focus and turned Slack into a collaboration platform for teams, which quickly became a massive success.

Conclusion:

Ignoring customer feedback is a recipe for product failure. By actively seeking and incorporating customer feedback into your product development process, you can build products that truly meet the needs of your users, foster loyalty, and drive long-term success. Remember, your customers are your most valuable asset. Their insights and opinions are essential for creating products that they will love and that will ultimately benefit your business.

11.3 Overpromising and Underdelivering: The Trap of Unrealistic Expectations

In the eagerness to excite stakeholders and customers, product managers can sometimes fall into the trap of overpromising and underdelivering. This can manifest in various forms, such as committing to unrealistic deadlines, exaggerating the capabilities of a feature, or promising a seamless user experience that is ultimately riddled with bugs and glitches.

The allure of setting ambitious goals and painting a rosy picture of the product's potential is understandable. It can generate excitement, secure buy-in, and even attract early adopters. However, when those promises are not met, the consequences can be severe.

The Fallout of Overpromising and Underdelivering:

- **Eroded Trust:** When you fail to deliver on your promises, it erodes trust with your team, stakeholders, and customers. This can make it difficult to gain support for future projects and initiatives.
- **Damaged Reputation:** A reputation for overpromising and underdelivering can tarnish your brand image and make it harder to attract new customers.
- **Increased Churn:** Users who feel misled or disappointed are more likely to abandon your product and switch to a competitor.

- **Financial Losses:** Underdelivering on features or delaying releases can lead to lost revenue, increased costs, and missed opportunities.
- **Demotivated Team:** When team members are constantly working under unrealistic expectations, it can lead to burnout, frustration, and decreased morale.

How to Avoid This Mistake:

1. **Set Realistic Expectations:** Be honest and transparent about what you can realistically achieve within the given timeframe and resources. Avoid making promises you cannot keep.
2. **Under-Promise and Over-Deliver:** It's better to set conservative estimates and then exceed them, rather than the other way around. This can create a positive surprise for your customers and stakeholders.
3. **Communicate Proactively:** Keep your team and stakeholders informed of progress, challenges, and any potential delays. Transparent communication can help manage expectations and build trust.
4. **Focus on Value Delivery:** Prioritize features and improvements that deliver the most value to customers, even if it means scaling back on less impactful features.
5. **Build in Buffer Time:** Incorporate buffer time into your project plans to account for unexpected delays or challenges.
6. **Say No When Necessary:** Don't be afraid to say no to requests or features that are not feasible or aligned with your product strategy.
7. **Manage Scope Creep:** Be vigilant about scope creep and ensure that the project stays focused on the agreed-upon goals and objectives.

Case Study: The Risks of Overpromising

In 2013, the healthcare startup HealthCare.gov launched a website to facilitate enrollment in health insurance plans under the Affordable Care Act. The website was plagued with technical problems from the start, leading to widespread frustration and criticism. The government had overpromised on the website's capabilities and timeline, leading to a public relations disaster and significant financial losses.

Conclusion:

Overpromising and underdelivering is a common trap that product managers must avoid. By setting realistic expectations, communicating proactively, focusing on value delivery, and managing scope creep, you can build trust with your team and stakeholders, deliver products that meet customer needs, and avoid the costly consequences of unmet promises.

11.4 Micromanaging the Team: Stifling Creativity and Growth

While a product manager's guidance and oversight are essential, there's a fine line between leadership and micromanagement. Micromanagement is the excessive control and supervision of employees' work, often involving a focus on minute details and a lack of trust in their abilities. It can manifest in various ways, such as constantly checking in on progress, second-guessing decisions, or insisting on doing things a specific way. While it may seem like a way to ensure quality and maintain control, micromanagement can have detrimental effects on both the team and the product.

The Pitfalls of Micromanagement:

- Stifled Creativity and Innovation: When team members feel constantly monitored and second-guessed, they become hesitant to take risks, experiment with new ideas, or think outside the box. This can stifle creativity and innovation, which are essential for building successful products.
- Demotivated and Disengaged Employees: Micromanagement creates an environment of distrust and lack of autonomy. This can lead to demotivation, resentment, and disengagement among team members, ultimately impacting productivity and morale.
- Increased Turnover: Employees who feel micromanaged are more likely to seek opportunities elsewhere, leading to higher turnover rates and the loss of valuable talent.
- Bottlenecks and Delays: When a product manager insists on making all the decisions and controlling every detail, it can create bottlenecks and slow down the development process.
- Missed Opportunities: Micromanagement can prevent team members from identifying and seizing opportunities, as they may be too focused on following instructions and avoiding mistakes.

How to Avoid Micromanagement:

1. Trust Your Team: Hire talented individuals and trust them to do their jobs. Delegate tasks, empower them to make decisions, and provide them with the resources and support they need to succeed.
2. Set Clear Expectations: Clearly define roles and responsibilities, establish goals and objectives, and communicate expectations clearly. This will help

team members understand what is expected of them and give them the autonomy to work independently.

3. Focus on Outcomes, Not Processes: Instead of dictating how things should be done, focus on the desired outcomes. Give your team the flexibility to figure out the best way to achieve those outcomes.

4. Provide Regular Feedback: Offer regular feedback on performance, both positive and constructive. This will help team members understand how they are doing and identify areas for improvement.

5. Encourage Open Communication: Create a safe space for team members to share ideas, concerns, and feedback. Encourage open dialogue and collaboration to foster a sense of ownership and shared responsibility.

6. Delegate and Empower: Don't be afraid to delegate tasks and responsibilities. Empower your team members to take ownership of their work and make decisions within their areas of expertise.

7. Let Go of Control: Recognize that you cannot control every detail. Trust your team to make the right decisions and learn from their mistakes.

Case Study: The Benefits of Empowering Teams

Consider the case of Google, a company renowned for its innovative products and services. Google fosters a culture of empowerment, encouraging employees to take risks, experiment with new ideas, and challenge the status quo. This has led to the development of groundbreaking products like Gmail, Google Maps, and Android.

By contrast, companies that micromanage their employees often stifle creativity and innovation. This can lead to a lack of new product ideas, a decline in market share, and ultimately, a loss of competitiveness.

Conclusion:

Micromanagement is a destructive behavior that can have a devastating impact on team morale, productivity, and innovation. By trusting your team, setting clear expectations, focusing on outcomes, and encouraging open communication, you can create a more empowering and collaborative environment where creativity and innovation can thrive.

11.5 Neglecting Data and Analytics: Flying Blind in the Digital Age

In the era of big data, where information is readily available and insights are abundant, neglecting data and analytics is akin to flying blind. Product managers who rely solely on intuition, gut feelings, or anecdotal evidence are missing out on a wealth of valuable information that can inform their decisions, drive product improvement, and ultimately lead to greater success.

The Dangers of Neglecting Data and Analytics:

- Misinformed Decisions: Without data, product managers are forced to rely on guesswork and assumptions, which can lead to misguided decisions that harm the product's development and performance.
- Missed Opportunities: Data can reveal hidden patterns, trends, and customer preferences that can unlock new opportunities for innovation and growth. Neglecting data means missing out on these valuable insights.
- Inefficient Resource Allocation: Without data to guide resource allocation, product managers may invest in features or initiatives that don't resonate

with users or deliver value, leading to wasted resources and missed deadlines.

- Unclear Impact Measurement: Data provides the means to measure the impact of your product decisions and initiatives. Without it, you'll struggle to determine what's working and what's not, hindering your ability to optimize and improve your product.
- Falling Behind the Competition: Competitors who leverage data and analytics gain a significant advantage. They can make faster, more informed decisions, identify emerging trends, and adapt quickly to changing market conditions.

How to Avoid This Mistake:

1. Embrace Data-Driven Decision Making: Make data an integral part of your product management process. Use data to validate assumptions, prioritize features, measure progress, and inform your overall product strategy.
2. Invest in Analytics and Tracking Tools: Utilize robust analytics platforms to track user behavior, engagement, and conversion. Implement tracking mechanisms to collect relevant data points that align with your KPIs.
3. Build a Data-Literate Team: Ensure that your team members have the skills and knowledge to interpret and use data effectively. Provide training and resources to foster a data-driven culture within your organization.
4. Focus on Actionable Insights: Don't get bogged down in the sheer volume of data. Focus on extracting actionable insights that can be used to improve your product and drive business outcomes.

5. Experiment and Iterate: Use data to test hypotheses, experiment with different approaches, and learn from your successes and failures.

Case Study: The Power of Data-Driven Insights

Netflix is a prime example of a company that leverages data and analytics to drive product success. They collect massive amounts of data on user behavior, including what they watch, when they watch, and how they rate content. This data is used to power their recommendation engine, personalize the user experience, and inform their content acquisition and production decisions. By harnessing the power of data, Netflix has become a global leader in streaming entertainment.

Conclusion:

In today's data-driven world, neglecting data and analytics is a recipe for failure. By embracing a data-driven approach to product management, you can gain valuable insights, make informed decisions, and build products that truly resonate with your users.

11.6 Resisting Change and Failing to Adapt: The Perils of Stagnation

The software industry is a dynamic landscape, characterized by constant innovation, shifting user preferences, and emerging technologies. In this ever-changing environment, resisting change and failing to adapt can be a fatal mistake for product managers. A rigid adherence to outdated strategies, technologies, or processes can lead to stagnation, rendering your product irrelevant and uncompetitive in the market.

The Risks of Resisting Change:

- **Missed Opportunities:** The tech world is full of opportunities for those who are willing to embrace change and innovation. By resisting change, you may miss out on emerging trends, new technologies, or shifts in customer preferences that could propel your product forward.
- **Loss of Relevance:** Customers expect products to evolve and improve over time. If your product stagnates, it will quickly lose its appeal and become outdated compared to more innovative competitors.
- **Declining Market Share:** As your product becomes less relevant, you'll likely see a decline in market share as customers flock to more up-to-date and feature-rich alternatives.
- **Demotivated Team:** A stagnant product can demotivate your team, as they see their hard work becoming less impactful and their creative potential stifled.

How to Avoid This Mistake:

1. **Embrace a Growth Mindset:** Cultivate a growth mindset within yourself and your team. Encourage a willingness to learn, experiment, and embrace new ideas.
2. **Stay Informed:** Keep abreast of the latest trends, technologies, and best practices in your industry. Attend conferences, read industry publications, and network with other professionals to stay informed and inspired.
3. **Encourage Experimentation:** Create a safe space for your team to experiment with new ideas and approaches. Don't be afraid to try new things, even if they don't always succeed.

4. **Gather Feedback Continuously:** Regularly seek feedback from customers, stakeholders, and your team to identify areas for improvement and opportunities for innovation.
5. **Iterate and Adapt:** Embrace an iterative approach to product development, continuously refining and improving your product based on feedback and data.
6. **Be Proactive, Not Reactive:** Don't wait for the market to force your hand. Anticipate change, identify emerging trends, and proactively adapt your product strategy and roadmap.
7. **Foster a Culture of Continuous Improvement:** Create an environment where continuous learning and improvement are valued and rewarded. Encourage your team to challenge assumptions, question the status quo, and seek out new ways to improve the product.

Case Study: The Power of Adaptation

Consider the example of Microsoft. In the early 2000s, Microsoft was dominant in the personal computing market with its Windows operating system and Office suite. However, they were slow to adapt to the rise of mobile devices and cloud computing, leading to a decline in market share and relevance.

However, under the leadership of Satya Nadella, Microsoft embraced a new vision of "mobile-first, cloud-first," transforming its business model and product portfolio to focus on cloud services and mobile productivity tools. This bold shift allowed Microsoft to regain its footing in the market and become a leader in the cloud computing space.

Conclusion:

The ability to adapt to change is not just a desirable trait for product managers; it is a survival imperative in the fast-paced world of software. By embracing change, staying informed, encouraging experimentation, and fostering a culture of continuous improvement, you can ensure that your product remains relevant, competitive, and successful in the long run.

11.7 Lack of Communication and Collaboration: Building Silos, Not Products

In the complex ecosystem of software product development, effective communication and collaboration are not merely desirable; they are essential. A product manager who fails to foster open lines of communication and create a collaborative environment risks building silos instead of products.

The Perils of Poor Communication and Collaboration:

- **Misaligned Goals and Priorities:** When teams work in isolation, their goals and priorities may diverge, leading to conflicts, delays, and a product that fails to meet the needs of all stakeholders.
- **Duplication of Effort:** Lack of communication can result in teams working on similar tasks or features without realizing it, wasting valuable time and resources.
- **Missed Opportunities for Innovation:** Collaboration sparks creativity and fosters innovation. When teams don't communicate openly, they miss out on opportunities to leverage each other's expertise and insights to generate new ideas and solutions.

- **Slower Decision-Making:** When communication is poor, decisions can get bogged down in bureaucracy and delays, hindering the product's progress.
- **Decreased Morale and Productivity:** A lack of communication and collaboration can create a toxic work environment, leading to frustration, resentment, and decreased morale among team members.

How to Avoid This Mistake:

1. **Establish Clear Communication Channels:** Create a variety of communication channels to facilitate both formal and informal communication. This could include regular team meetings, one-on-one check-ins, instant messaging platforms, and project management tools.
2. **Encourage Open and Transparent Communication:** Foster a culture where team members feel comfortable sharing ideas, asking questions, and voicing concerns. Encourage open dialogue and create a safe space for constructive feedback.
3. **Set Clear Expectations and Roles:** Clearly define the roles and responsibilities of each team member, and ensure that everyone understands how their work contributes to the overall product goals.
4. **Promote Cross-Functional Collaboration:** Encourage collaboration between different departments and teams. Create opportunities for cross-functional teams to work together on projects and share knowledge and expertise.
5. **Use Collaborative Tools:** Leverage project management tools, communication platforms, and document-sharing tools to facilitate collaboration and information sharing.

6. **Celebrate Successes Together:** Recognize and celebrate the achievements of the team as a whole, rather than just individual contributions. This will foster a sense of shared purpose and camaraderie.

Case Study: The Power of Collaboration

The development of the iPhone is a prime example of the power of collaboration. The iPhone was not created by a single individual or department; it was the result of a collaborative effort between designers, engineers, marketers, and executives, all working together to create a groundbreaking product that revolutionized the mobile industry.

Conclusion:

Communication and collaboration are not just soft skills; they are essential competencies for successful product management. By fostering open communication, building trust, and encouraging collaboration, you can create a high-performing team that is capable of delivering exceptional products.

11.8 Focusing on Features Over Benefits: Missing the Forest for the Trees

A common pitfall for product managers is becoming overly enamored with features and losing sight of the benefits those features provide to users. This can lead to a product that is technically impressive but lacks the emotional resonance and practical value that truly connects with customers. It's like building a house with all the latest gadgets and gizmos but forgetting to make it a comfortable and welcoming home.

The Trap of Feature Obsession:

- **Complexity and Bloat:** A product packed with features can become overly complex and difficult to use, overwhelming users and hindering adoption.
- **Irrelevant Features:** Focusing on features that don't align with user needs or pain points results in wasted development effort and a product that feels disjointed.
- **Lack of Clarity:** When you focus on features rather than benefits, your marketing messages become a laundry list of technical specifications instead of a compelling story about how the product solves problems and improves lives.
- **Missed Opportunities for Differentiation:** Competitors can easily replicate features, but it's much harder to replicate the unique value and benefits that a product delivers.
- **Lower Customer Satisfaction:** Users ultimately care about how a product makes them feel and the problems it solves, not just the list of features it boasts.

How to Avoid This Mistake:

1. **Shift Your Focus to Benefits:** Start by understanding the core benefits your product delivers to users. What problems does it solve? How does it improve their lives or work? Focus on communicating these benefits in your marketing and product messaging.
2. **Prioritize User Needs:** Conduct thorough user research to understand their needs, pain points, and desired outcomes. Prioritize features that directly address these needs and deliver tangible benefits.

3. **Tell a Compelling Story:** Craft a narrative around your product that highlights the benefits it delivers and the positive impact it has on users' lives. Use customer testimonials, case studies, and demos to illustrate these benefits.
4. **Simplify and Streamline:** Don't overload your product with unnecessary features. Focus on a few core features that deliver the most value and make the user experience as simple and intuitive as possible.
5. **Highlight the "Why":** Explain why your product is different and better than the competition. Don't just list features; articulate the unique value proposition that sets your product apart.

Case Study: The Importance of Benefits over Features

Consider the example of Dropbox. When it first launched, Dropbox wasn't the only cloud storage solution on the market. However, it quickly gained popularity due to its focus on simplicity and ease of use. Instead of overwhelming users with a plethora of features, Dropbox focused on the core benefit of providing a seamless way to store, sync, and share files across devices. This user-centric approach resonated with customers and propelled Dropbox to become a leading player in the cloud storage industry.

Conclusion:

Focusing on features over benefits is a common mistake that can lead to product failure. By shifting your focus to the benefits your product delivers, prioritizing user needs, and simplifying your messaging, you can create a product that not only meets the functional requirements of users but also resonates with them on an emotional level, driving adoption, loyalty, and long-term success.

11.9 Ignoring the Competition: A Blind Spot in Your Product Strategy

In the fiercely competitive software market, ignoring your competition is like playing a game of chess without looking at the board. Your competitors are not static entities; they are constantly evolving, innovating, and vying for the same customers as you. Neglecting to analyze and understand their strategies, strengths, and weaknesses can leave you vulnerable and ill-prepared to defend your market position.

The Risks of Ignoring the Competition:

- **Missed Threats:** Competitors may be developing new features, entering new markets, or forming strategic partnerships that could undermine your product's position. By ignoring them, you risk being caught off guard and losing market share.
- **Lack of Differentiation:** Without understanding what sets your competitors apart, you may struggle to differentiate your own product and articulate a unique value proposition that resonates with customers.
- **Missed Opportunities:** Competitors can sometimes offer valuable lessons and insights. By studying their successes and failures, you can identify potential opportunities for innovation, improvement, and market expansion.
- **Underestimating Challenges:** Ignoring the competition can lead to a false sense of security, causing you to underestimate the challenges and obstacles you may face in the market.
- **Losing the Competitive Edge:** In today's fast-paced market, standing still is not an option. By failing to keep up with the competition, you risk

losing your competitive edge and becoming irrelevant.

How to Avoid This Mistake:

1. **Conduct Regular Competitive Analysis:** Make competitive analysis an ongoing part of your product management process. Regularly assess the landscape, identify key competitors, and analyze their products, strategies, and positioning.
2. **Understand Your Competitors' Strengths and Weaknesses:** Identify the areas where your competitors excel and where they fall short. This will help you to identify opportunities for differentiation and areas where you can improve your own product.
3. **Monitor Market Trends:** Stay abreast of the latest trends and developments in your industry. This will help you to anticipate changes in the competitive landscape and adapt your strategy accordingly.
4. **Learn from Your Competitors:** Don't be afraid to learn from your competitors. Study their successes and failures to gain insights that can inform your own product decisions.
5. **Differentiate Your Product:** Clearly articulate what sets your product apart from the competition. Focus on your unique value proposition, key differentiators, and the benefits you offer to customers.

Case Study: The Importance of Staying Ahead of the Competition

The rivalry between Apple and Samsung in the smartphone market is a classic example of the importance of understanding and responding to the competition. Both companies constantly monitor each other's moves, launching new products and features to stay ahead of the curve. This fierce competition has driven innovation in the smartphone industry, benefiting consumers with better products and more choices.

Conclusion:

Ignoring the competition is a recipe for complacency and decline. By actively monitoring your competitors, understanding their strengths and weaknesses, and differentiating your product, you can stay ahead of the curve, anticipate market shifts, and maintain a competitive edge.

Common Mistakes to Avoid in Product Management Action List

1. **Define a Clear Vision and Strategy:**

- Craft a compelling vision statement: Articulate the long-term goal and desired impact of your product.
- Develop a comprehensive product strategy: Outline your target market, value proposition, differentiators, go-to-market strategy, and roadmap.
- Communicate clearly and regularly: Ensure your team and stakeholders understand the vision and strategy.
- Align with business goals: Make sure your product roadmap supports the overall business objectives.
- Measure progress with data: Track key metrics to assess your progress and identify areas for improvement.

2. **Prioritize Customer Feedback and Needs:**

- Actively seek feedback: Create multiple channels for gathering feedback, such as surveys, interviews, and user testing.
- Listen actively and empathetically: Understand the underlying needs and motivations behind customer feedback.
- Involve customers in the development process: Invite them to participate in beta testing, user research, and focus groups.
- Analyze and act on feedback: Regularly review feedback and use it to inform your product roadmap and decisions.
- Close the feedback loop: Communicate back to customers how their feedback has been incorporated.

3. **Set Realistic Expectations and Deliver on Promises:**

- Under-promise and over-deliver: Set conservative estimates and strive to exceed them.
- Communicate proactively: Keep stakeholders informed of progress, challenges, and potential delays.
- Focus on value delivery: Prioritize features that provide the most value to customers.
- Build in buffer time: Incorporate extra time in your project plans to account for unforeseen issues.
- Say no when necessary: Don't be afraid to turn down requests that are not feasible or aligned with your strategy.
- Manage scope creep: Keep the project focused on the agreed-upon goals and objectives.

4. **Avoid Micromanaging Your Team:**

- Trust your team: Hire talented individuals and empower them to do their jobs.
- Set clear expectations: Define roles, responsibilities, goals, and performance expectations.
- Focus on outcomes: Give your team the autonomy to figure out the best way to achieve desired results.
- Provide regular feedback: Offer both positive and constructive feedback to help team members grow.
- Encourage open communication: Create a safe space for sharing ideas, concerns, and feedback.
- Delegate and empower: Trust your team to make decisions and learn from their mistakes.

5. **Leverage Data and Analytics:**

- Embrace data-driven decision-making: Use data to validate assumptions, measure progress, and inform your strategy.
- Invest in analytics tools: Utilize platforms to track user behavior, engagement, and conversion.
- Build a data-literate team: Ensure your team members understand how to interpret and use data effectively.
- Focus on actionable insights: Extract meaningful insights from data that can drive product improvements.
- Experiment and iterate: Use data to test hypotheses and continuously refine your approach.

6. **Embrace Change and Adapt:**

- Foster a growth mindset: Encourage a willingness to learn, experiment, and embrace new ideas.
- Stay informed: Keep up with industry trends, technologies, and best practices.

- Encourage experimentation: Create a safe space for your team to try new things and learn from failures.
- Gather feedback continuously: Seek input from customers, stakeholders, and your team to identify areas for improvement.
- Iterate and adapt: Continuously refine your product and strategy based on feedback and data.

7. **Foster Open Communication and Collaboration:**

- Establish clear communication channels: Use a variety of channels, including meetings, messaging, and project management tools.
- Encourage open dialogue: Create a safe space for sharing ideas, concerns, and feedback.
- Set clear expectations and roles: Define responsibilities and ensure everyone understands their role in the team.
- Promote cross-functional collaboration: Encourage teams from different departments to work together and share knowledge.
- Celebrate successes together: Recognize and celebrate the achievements of the entire team.

8. **Focus on Benefits Over Features:**

- Understand user needs: Conduct thorough user research to identify pain points and desired outcomes.
- Prioritize benefits: Focus on the value your product delivers to users, not just the features it offers.
- Tell a compelling story: Craft a narrative that highlights the benefits and impact of your product.
- Simplify and streamline: Avoid overloading your product with unnecessary features.

- Highlight your unique value proposition: Clearly articulate what sets your product apart from the competition.

9. **Don't Ignore the Competition:**

- Conduct regular competitive analysis: Assess the market landscape, identify key competitors, and analyze their products and strategies.
- Understand their strengths and weaknesses: Identify areas where you can differentiate and improve.
- Monitor market trends: Stay ahead of the curve by anticipating changes in the competitive landscape.
- Learn from your competitors: Study their successes and failures to gain valuable insights.
- Differentiate your product: Clearly articulate your unique value proposition and key differentiators.

By avoiding these common mistakes and implementing the recommended actions, you can significantly increase your chances of building successful products that meet customer needs, achieve business objectives, and stand the test of time.

Chapter 12: Legal and Regulatory Considerations: Navigating the Compliance Landscape

Software product management is not just about building great products; it's also about navigating a complex and ever-changing landscape of legal and regulatory requirements. As software becomes increasingly integrated into our lives and businesses, governments and regulatory bodies are enacting laws and regulations to protect consumers, ensure fair competition, and safeguard sensitive data.

For product managers, understanding and complying with these legal and regulatory considerations is not just a matter of avoiding fines or penalties; it's a critical aspect of building trust with customers, mitigating risks, and ensuring the long-term sustainability of your product. This chapter will delve into the key legal and regulatory areas that product managers need to be aware of, providing an overview of the relevant laws, regulations, and best practices for ensuring compliance.

In this chapter, you will:

- **Understand the importance of legal and regulatory compliance in product management:** Learn how compliance can protect your company, your customers, and your product's reputation.
- **Explore key legal areas relevant to software products:** Gain insights into intellectual property rights, data privacy regulations, software licensing, export controls, and accessibility laws.
- **Learn about best practices for ensuring compliance:** Discover strategies for conducting risk

assessments, implementing compliance programs, and staying up-to-date on evolving regulations.

By navigating the legal and regulatory landscape with knowledge and diligence, you can build products that not only meet user needs but also adhere to the highest ethical and legal standards. This chapter will equip you with the knowledge and tools you need to create responsible and compliant products that can stand the test of time.

12.1 Intellectual Property and Patent Protection: Safeguarding Your Innovations

Intellectual property (IP) is the lifeblood of software companies. It encompasses the creative and innovative ideas, processes, and expressions that differentiate your product from the competition. Protecting your intellectual property is crucial for maintaining a competitive edge, attracting investors, and ensuring the long-term success of your business.

Types of Intellectual Property Protection for Software:

1. **Copyright:** This automatically protects the expression of your software code, user interface, and documentation from unauthorized copying or distribution. While registration with the U.S. Copyright Office is not mandatory, it provides additional legal benefits, such as the ability to sue for statutory damages and attorney's fees.
2. **Patents:** Patents protect the underlying inventions or processes embodied in your software. They grant you the exclusive right to make, use, sell, or import your invention for a limited period, typically 20 years from the filing date. Obtaining a patent requires a rigorous examination process to ensure

that your invention is novel, non-obvious, and useful.

3. **Trade Secrets:** This protects confidential information that gives your company a competitive advantage, such as source code, algorithms, customer lists, or marketing strategies. Unlike patents and copyrights, trade secrets are not registered with the government. Instead, you must take reasonable steps to keep the information confidential, such as using non-disclosure agreements (NDAs) and limiting access to authorized personnel.

4. **Trademarks:** Trademarks protect words, phrases, symbols, or designs that identify and distinguish your product from others in the market. Registering your trademark with the U.S. Patent and Trademark Office (USPTO) gives you the exclusive right to use the mark in connection with your goods or services.

Strategies for Protecting Your Intellectual Property:

- **Identify Your IP Assets:** Take an inventory of your intellectual property assets, including software code, user interfaces, designs, algorithms, data, and trade secrets.
- **Develop an IP Strategy:** Create a comprehensive IP strategy that outlines how you will protect, manage, and leverage your IP assets.
- **Secure Appropriate Protection:** Determine the best type of IP protection for each asset. This may involve filing for patents, registering copyrights or trademarks, or taking steps to protect trade secrets.
- **Use Contracts and Agreements:** Use contracts and agreements, such as NDAs, employment agreements, and licensing agreements, to protect your IP rights and prevent unauthorized use.

- **Monitor and Enforce Your Rights:** Regularly monitor the market for potential infringement of your IP rights and take action to enforce them when necessary.

Best Practices for IP Protection:

- **Document Your Innovations:** Keep detailed records of your inventions, including notes, drawings, prototypes, and test results.
- **Mark Your IP:** Use copyright notices, patent numbers, and trademark symbols to indicate your ownership of your intellectual property.
- **Educate Your Employees:** Educate your employees about your IP policies and the importance of protecting confidential information.
- **Seek Legal Counsel:** Consult with an intellectual property attorney to get advice on the best strategies for protecting your specific IP assets.

Conclusion:

Protecting your intellectual property is a critical aspect of software product management. By taking proactive steps to secure your IP rights, you can safeguard your innovations, deter infringement, and build a sustainable competitive advantage. Remember, your intellectual property is a valuable asset that deserves to be protected.

12.2 Data Privacy and Security Regulations (GDPR, CCPA, etc.): Protecting User Data in the Digital Age

In an era where data is often referred to as the "new oil," protecting the privacy and security of user data has become a paramount concern for businesses and product managers alike. With the rise of data breaches, identity theft, and other cyber threats, governments and regulatory bodies worldwide have enacted stringent data privacy and security regulations to safeguard personal information and hold organizations accountable for their data practices.

Understanding and complying with these regulations is not only a legal obligation but also a critical aspect of building trust with your customers and ensuring the long-term success of your product. This subchapter will explore the key data privacy and security regulations that impact software product management, highlighting their requirements, implications, and best practices for compliance.

General Data Protection Regulation (GDPR):

Enacted by the European Union (EU) in 2018, the GDPR is one of the most comprehensive and far-reaching data privacy laws in the world. It applies to any organization that processes the personal data of EU residents, regardless of the organization's location.

Key GDPR requirements:

- **Lawful Basis for Processing:** Organizations must have a lawful basis for collecting and processing personal data, such as consent, contract, legal obligation, vital interests, public task, or legitimate interests.
- **Data Subject Rights:** Individuals have the right to access, rectify, erase, restrict processing, data portability, and object to the processing of their personal data.

- **Privacy by Design and Default:** Organizations must implement appropriate technical and organizational measures to protect personal data from unauthorized access, disclosure, alteration, or destruction.
- **Data Breach Notification:** Organizations must notify the relevant authorities and affected individuals of any data breaches within 72 hours of becoming aware of the breach.

California Consumer Privacy Act (CCPA):

The CCPA, enacted in California in 2020, is a landmark privacy law in the United States that grants California residents certain rights over their personal information collected by businesses.

Key CCPA requirements:

- **Right to Know:** Consumers have the right to know what personal information businesses collect about them, how it is used, and whether it is sold or disclosed to third parties.
- **Right to Delete:** Consumers can request that businesses delete their personal information.
- **Right to Opt-Out:** Consumers can opt out of the sale of their personal information.
- **Non-Discrimination:** Businesses cannot discriminate against consumers who exercise their rights under the CCPA.

Other Data Privacy Regulations:

In addition to the GDPR and CCPA, there are numerous other data privacy laws and regulations around the world, such as the Personal Information Protection and Electronic

Documents Act (PIPEDA) in Canada, the Lei Geral de Proteção de Dados Pessoais (LGPD) in Brazil, and the Personal Data Protection Act (PDPA) in Singapore.

Best Practices for Compliance:

- **Conduct a Privacy Impact Assessment (PIA):** Assess the potential privacy risks of your product and develop strategies to mitigate them.
- **Implement Privacy by Design:** Incorporate privacy considerations into the design of your product from the outset.
- **Obtain Explicit Consent:** Obtain clear and informed consent from users before collecting or processing their personal data.
- **Provide Transparency:** Be transparent about your data collection and processing practices, and give users control over their data.
- **Secure User Data:** Implement appropriate security measures to protect user data from unauthorized access, disclosure, alteration, or destruction.
- **Train Employees:** Educate your employees about data privacy regulations and your company's policies.
- **Stay Informed:** Stay up-to-date on the latest developments in data privacy laws and regulations, and adapt your practices accordingly.

By understanding and complying with data privacy and security regulations, you can protect your users' data, build trust with your customers, and avoid costly fines and penalties. Compliance is not just a legal requirement; it is a business imperative for the long-term success of your product.

12.3 Software Licensing and Compliance: Navigating the Permissions Maze

Software licensing is a legal instrument that governs the use and distribution of software. It defines the terms and conditions under which a user can access, install, use, copy, modify, or redistribute the software. Product managers must understand the different types of software licenses and ensure that their products are distributed and used in compliance with the terms of the license.

Types of Software Licenses:

1. **Proprietary Licenses:** These licenses grant limited rights to the user, typically restricting the use to a specific number of devices or users. They often prohibit copying, modifying, or redistributing the software. Examples include Microsoft Windows and Adobe Photoshop.
2. **Open Source Licenses:** These licenses grant users the freedom to use, modify, and distribute the software, often with the requirement that any modifications or derivative works are also released under the same open-source license. Examples include the GNU General Public License (GPL) and the MIT License.
3. **Freeware Licenses:** These licenses allow users to use the software for free, but they may have restrictions on commercial use or distribution. Examples include Skype and Adobe Reader.
4. **Shareware Licenses:** These licenses allow users to try the software for free for a limited period or with limited functionality. To continue using the software beyond the trial period or to unlock full functionality, users must purchase a license.

5. **Creative Commons Licenses:** These licenses offer a flexible framework for copyright holders to grant others permission to use their work under specific conditions. They are often used for creative works, such as images, music, and videos.

Software Licensing Compliance:

Product managers are responsible for ensuring that their products are distributed and used in compliance with the terms of the license. This includes:

- **Choosing the Right License:** Selecting a license that aligns with your business goals and the intended use of the software.
- **Drafting Clear License Agreements:** Creating clear and concise license agreements that outline the terms and conditions of use.
- **Ensuring Compliance Throughout the Product Lifecycle:** Monitoring the distribution and use of the software to ensure that it complies with the license terms.
- **Educating Users:** Providing clear instructions and documentation to users on how to use the software in compliance with the license.
- **Taking Action Against Infringement:** If necessary, taking legal action against users who violate the terms of the license.

Best Practices for Software Licensing Compliance:

- **Seek Legal Counsel:** Consult with an attorney specializing in software licensing to ensure that your license agreements are legally sound and enforceable.

- **Regularly Review and Update Licenses:** Keep your license agreements up-to-date to reflect changes in the law or your business practices.
- **Implement a License Management System:** Use a license management system to track licenses, monitor usage, and enforce compliance.
- **Provide Clear and Accessible Licensing Information:** Make your license agreements easily accessible to users and provide clear instructions on how to comply with the terms.
- **Educate Your Team:** Train your employees on software licensing compliance and the importance of protecting your intellectual property.

By understanding the intricacies of software licensing and implementing best practices for compliance, product managers can protect their intellectual property, mitigate legal risks, and ensure that their products are used ethically and responsibly.

12.4 Export Controls and Trade Restrictions: Navigating International Boundaries

Software, despite its intangible nature, is not immune to the constraints of international borders. Export controls and trade restrictions are governmental regulations that restrict the flow of certain goods, technologies, and information across national boundaries. These regulations are enacted to protect national security, foreign policy interests, and economic stability. For product managers developing software with potential international reach, understanding and adhering to these regulations is crucial to avoid legal repercussions and ensure smooth global operations.

Understanding Export Controls:

Export controls primarily govern the transfer of technology, software, and information that can have dual-use applications, meaning they can be used for both civilian and military purposes. These controls are often based on the nature of the technology, the destination country, the end-user, and the intended use.

Key Export Control Regulations:

- **Export Administration Regulations (EAR):** Administered by the Bureau of Industry and Security (BIS), the EAR regulates the export and re-export of most commercial goods, software, and technology. It classifies items based on their technical characteristics and the destination country, determining whether a license is required for export.
- **International Traffic in Arms Regulations (ITAR):** Administered by the Directorate of Defense Trade Controls (DDTC), the ITAR regulates the export of defense articles and services, including military software and technology. It imposes stricter controls than the EAR and requires licenses for most exports.

Trade Restrictions:

In addition to export controls, product managers must also be aware of trade restrictions, such as sanctions and embargoes, which prohibit or limit trade with certain countries or individuals. These restrictions can be imposed for various reasons, including political instability, human rights abuses, or support for terrorism.

Implications for Product Managers:

Export controls and trade restrictions can have significant implications for software product managers:

- **Product Development:** Certain features or functionalities may need to be modified or removed to comply with export restrictions for specific countries.
- **Licensing and Distribution:** Product managers may need to obtain licenses for exporting their software to certain countries or restrict distribution to approved end-users.
- **Partnerships and Collaborations:** Collaborations with foreign entities may be subject to export control scrutiny, requiring due diligence and compliance measures.
- **Cloud Services:** If your software is hosted on cloud servers, you need to ensure that the data storage and processing comply with the export control regulations of the countries where the servers are located.

Best Practices for Compliance:

- **Classify Your Product:** Determine the appropriate export control classification for your software based on its technical characteristics and intended use.
- **Screen End-Users and Destinations:** Verify that your end-users and destinations are not prohibited or restricted parties under export control regulations.
- **Obtain Necessary Licenses:** If your software requires an export license, apply for and obtain the license before exporting.
- **Keep Records:** Maintain accurate records of your export transactions, including licenses, end-user information, and destination details.

- **Stay Informed:** Export control regulations are constantly evolving. Stay up-to-date on the latest changes and ensure that your practices remain compliant.
- **Seek Legal Counsel:** Consult with an attorney specializing in export controls to ensure that your product and business practices comply with all applicable regulations.

By understanding and adhering to export controls and trade restrictions, product managers can ensure that their software products can reach their full market potential while upholding legal and ethical obligations.

12.5 Accessibility and Disability Discrimination Laws: Building Inclusive Products for All

In an increasingly digital world, software products play a crucial role in how people work, learn, communicate, and access essential services. Ensuring that these products are accessible to individuals with disabilities is not only a legal imperative but also a moral responsibility and a business opportunity. This subchapter will delve into the laws and regulations that mandate accessibility, as well as the best practices for designing and developing products that are inclusive of all users.

Key Accessibility Laws and Regulations:

- **Americans with Disabilities Act (ADA):** Enacted in the United States in 1990, the ADA prohibits discrimination against individuals with disabilities in all areas of public life, including employment, transportation, public accommodations, communications, and access to state and local government programs and services. While not explicitly addressing digital accessibility, the ADA has been interpreted to apply to websites and mobile applications, requiring businesses to make their digital products accessible to people with disabilities.

- **Web Content Accessibility Guidelines (WCAG):** Developed by the World Wide Web Consortium (W3C), the WCAG are internationally recognized guidelines for making web content more accessible to people with disabilities. They provide a framework for designing and developing websites and applications that are perceivable, operable, understandable, and robust for users with various disabilities, such as visual, auditory, motor, and cognitive impairments.
- **Section 508 of the Rehabilitation Act:** This U.S. federal law requires federal agencies to make their electronic and information technology accessible to people with disabilities. It applies to all federal websites, applications, and other digital content.
- **Other Laws and Regulations:** Numerous other accessibility laws and regulations exist worldwide, such as the Accessibility for Ontarians with Disabilities Act (AODA) in Canada and the Equality Act 2010 in the United Kingdom.

Best Practices for Accessibility:

- **Incorporate Accessibility from the Start:** Consider accessibility from the earliest stages of product design and development. Involve people with disabilities in user research and testing to gain valuable insights into their needs and experiences.
- **Follow WCAG Guidelines:** Adhere to the WCAG guidelines, which provide detailed

recommendations for making web content accessible.

- **Use Accessible Design Patterns:** Utilize established design patterns and components that are known to be accessible, such as using sufficient color contrast, providing text alternatives for images, and ensuring keyboard navigation.
- **Conduct Accessibility Testing:** Regularly test your product with assistive technologies, such as screen readers and magnifiers, to identify and fix any accessibility issues.
- **Provide Accessibility Documentation:** Create clear and comprehensive documentation that explains how to use your product with assistive technologies.
- **Train Your Team:** Educate your team on accessibility principles and best practices.

Business Benefits of Accessibility:

- **Increased Market Reach:** By making your product accessible, you can tap into a larger market, including the estimated 1 billion people worldwide who have disabilities.
- **Improved Usability:** Accessible design often benefits all users, not just those with disabilities. For example, clear and concise content, intuitive navigation, and keyboard support can make your product easier to use for everyone.
- **Enhanced Brand Reputation:** Demonstrating a commitment to accessibility can enhance your brand reputation and build trust with customers.
- **Reduced Legal Risk:** Complying with accessibility laws can help you avoid costly lawsuits and penalties.

By prioritizing accessibility and inclusivity, product managers can build products that not only comply with legal requirements but also create a more equitable and inclusive digital landscape for all users. Embracing accessibility is not just a matter of social responsibility; it's a smart business strategy that can lead to increased customer satisfaction, expanded market reach, and long-term success.

Legal and Regulatory Considerations Action List:

1. **Intellectual Property (IP) Protection:**

   - Identify and inventory all IP assets: Software code, UI, designs, algorithms, data, trade secrets.
   - Develop a comprehensive IP strategy: Outline protection, management, and leverage of IP assets.
   - Secure appropriate protection: File for patents, register copyrights and trademarks, and establish safeguards for trade secrets.
   - Use contracts and agreements: Implement NDAs, employment agreements, and licensing agreements.
   - Monitor and enforce your rights: Regularly check for infringements and take legal action if necessary.

2. **Data Privacy and Security (GDPR, CCPA, etc.):**

   - Conduct Privacy Impact Assessments (PIA): Identify and mitigate privacy risks in your product.
   - Implement a data protection program: Establish policies, procedures, and training for employees on data handling.
   - Appoint a Data Protection Officer (DPO): If required, designate a DPO to oversee compliance.

- Review and update privacy policies: Ensure policies are current and transparent about data collection and use.
- Stay informed: Keep abreast of changes in data privacy regulations globally.

3. **Software Licensing and Compliance:**

- Choose the right license: Select a license that aligns with your business model and product usage.
- Draft clear license agreements: Create easy-to-understand terms and conditions for users.
- Ensure compliance: Monitor product distribution and use to maintain license adherence.
- Educate users: Provide clear instructions and documentation on compliant software usage.
- Address infringement: Take action against users who violate license terms.

4. **Export Controls and Trade Restrictions:**

- Classify your product: Determine its export control classification based on technical specifications and intended use.
- Screen end-users and destinations: Verify that they are not on any prohibited or restricted lists.
- Obtain necessary licenses: Apply for and secure any required export licenses before shipping.
- Keep meticulous records: Maintain detailed documentation of export transactions and licenses.
- Stay informed: Continuously monitor changes in export control regulations and adjust practices accordingly.
- Seek legal counsel: Consult with an expert in export controls for guidance on compliance.

5. **Accessibility and Disability Discrimination Laws:**

- Design for accessibility from the start: Integrate accessibility considerations throughout the product development process.
- Follow WCAG guidelines: Adhere to established guidelines for making web content accessible to all users.
- Use accessible design patterns: Implement user interface elements that cater to various disabilities.
- Conduct accessibility testing: Regularly test your product with assistive technologies to identify and fix issues.
- Provide documentation: Offer clear instructions on how to use your product with assistive technologies.
- Train your team: Educate team members on accessibility principles and best practices.

By diligently following this action list, product managers can ensure their software products navigate the legal and regulatory landscape successfully, minimizing risks and building trust with users and stakeholders.

Chapter 13: Budgeting and Financial Management: Ensuring Product Profitability

In the world of software product management, technical prowess and customer-centricity alone are not enough to guarantee success. A product, no matter how innovative or well-received, must also be financially viable. This chapter delves into the critical domain of budgeting and financial management, equipping product managers with the knowledge and tools needed to make sound financial decisions, optimize resource allocation, and ultimately ensure the profitability of their products.

Product managers are not just responsible for building great products; they are also accountable for their financial performance. This means understanding the costs associated with product development, forecasting revenue, tracking expenses, and ensuring that the product generates a return on investment (ROI) that justifies the resources invested. This chapter will explore the various aspects of budgeting and financial management, from developing a comprehensive product budget to forecasting revenue and expenses, tracking financial performance, managing costs, and optimizing resources.

In this chapter, you will:

- **Learn how to develop a product budget:** Understand the different types of costs involved in product development and how to create a budget that aligns with your product strategy and financial goals.
- **Master the art of forecasting revenue and expenses:** Learn techniques for predicting future

revenue streams and estimating expenses to ensure your product is financially sustainable.

- **Track and analyze financial performance:** Utilize financial metrics and reporting tools to monitor your product's financial health and identify areas for improvement.
- **Manage costs and optimize resources:** Discover strategies for controlling costs, optimizing resource allocation, and maximizing the value of your investments.
- **Calculate return on investment (ROI):** Understand how to measure the financial performance of your product and evaluate its overall profitability.

By mastering the principles of budgeting and financial management, product managers can make informed decisions that drive product success and profitability. This chapter will provide you with the knowledge and tools you need to navigate the financial complexities of product development and ensure that your products are not only innovative and user-friendly but also financially viable.

13.1 Developing a Product Budget: Mapping the Financial Terrain

A well-structured budget is the financial backbone of any software product. It serves as a roadmap for resource allocation, cost control, and revenue generation, ensuring that your product can be developed, launched, and maintained profitably. Developing a product budget requires careful planning, realistic estimation, and ongoing monitoring to ensure that your project stays on track and delivers a positive return on investment (ROI).

Key Components of a Product Budget:

1. Development Costs:

- **Personnel:** Salaries, benefits, and bonuses for the development team (engineers, designers, QA testers, etc.).
- **Technology:** Software licenses, cloud infrastructure costs, development tools, and hardware expenses.
- **Contractors and Consultants:** Fees for external contractors or consultants who provide specialized skills or services.
- **Prototyping and Testing:** Costs associated with creating prototypes, conducting user research, and performing quality assurance testing.
- **Training:** Expenses for training the development team on new technologies or processes.

2. Marketing and Sales Costs:

- **Market Research:** Costs associated with conducting market research, analyzing competitor offerings, and identifying target customer segments.
- **Marketing and Advertising:** Expenses for creating and executing marketing campaigns, including advertising, social media, content marketing, and public relations.
- **Sales:** Salaries, commissions, and bonuses for the sales team, as well as travel expenses and sales tools.
- **Channel Partner Costs:** If you are working with channel partners or resellers, you may need to budget for channel marketing support, commissions, and training.

3. Operational Costs:

- **Hosting and Infrastructure:** Costs associated with hosting your software, including server costs, bandwidth, and data storage.
- **Maintenance and Support:** Expenses for ongoing maintenance, bug fixes, updates, and customer support.
- **Professional Services:** If you offer professional services, such as custom development or implementation, you'll need to factor in the costs associated with delivering those services.

4. Contingency Costs:

- It's essential to include a contingency buffer in your budget to account for unexpected expenses or delays. This buffer should typically be 10-20% of your overall budget.

Steps for Developing a Product Budget:

1. Define the Scope of the Project: Clearly outline the features, functionalities, and deliverables of your product. This will help you estimate the resources and costs required for each phase of development.
2. Estimate Costs: Work with your team to estimate the costs associated with each component of your budget. Use historical data, industry benchmarks, and vendor quotes to arrive at realistic estimates.
3. Prioritize and Allocate Resources: Prioritize the most important features and allocate resources accordingly. Be prepared to make trade-offs if your budget is limited.
4. Track and Monitor Expenses: Regularly track your expenses against your budget to ensure that you are staying on track. Identify any variances and take corrective action if necessary.

5. Review and Adjust: As your project progresses, review your budget regularly and make adjustments as needed. Be prepared to adapt to changing circumstances and unexpected costs.

Tips for Effective Budgeting:

- **Be Realistic:** Don't underestimate costs. Be honest and transparent about the resources required to build and launch your product.
- **Involve Stakeholders:** Get input from key stakeholders, including finance, marketing, and engineering teams, to ensure that your budget is comprehensive and realistic.
- **Use a Budgeting Tool:** Consider using a budgeting tool or software to help you create, track, and manage your budget.
- **Review Regularly:** Don't just set your budget and forget about it. Regularly review and update your budget to ensure it remains accurate and relevant.
- **Learn from Your Mistakes:** If you overspend or underestimate costs, analyze the reasons behind the variance and use that knowledge to improve your budgeting process for future projects.

By developing a well-structured and realistic budget, you can ensure that your product has the resources it needs to succeed, while also maintaining financial discipline and maximizing profitability.

13.2 Forecasting Revenue and Expenses: Predicting the Financial Future

In the dynamic world of software product management, forecasting revenue and expenses is a critical practice that allows you to anticipate the financial trajectory of your product, make informed decisions about resource allocation, and ensure the long-term sustainability of your business. Accurate forecasting enables you to identify potential risks and opportunities, set realistic goals, and track your progress towards profitability.

Forecasting Revenue:

Revenue forecasting involves estimating the amount of money your product will generate over a specific period. This can be a complex task, as it depends on numerous factors, including:

- **Market Size and Growth:** The overall size and growth potential of your target market.
- **Pricing Strategy:** Your pricing model, such as subscription-based, freemium, or tiered pricing.
- **Customer Acquisition and Retention Rates:** The rate at which you acquire new customers and retain existing ones.
- **Competitive Landscape:** The presence and strength of competitors in the market.
- **Sales and Marketing Efforts:** The effectiveness of your sales and marketing strategies in driving demand.
- **Economic Conditions:** The overall economic climate and its impact on consumer spending.

Methods for Forecasting Revenue:

- **Bottom-Up Forecasting:** This approach involves estimating revenue based on individual sales projections for specific products or customer segments.
- **Top-Down Forecasting:** This approach involves starting with a high-level estimate of the overall

market size and then narrowing it down to your expected market share.

- **Historical Data Analysis:** This involves analyzing past sales data to identify trends and patterns that can be used to predict future revenue.
- **Market Research:** Conducting market research to gather data on customer preferences, willingness to pay, and competitive pricing.

Forecasting Expenses:

Expense forecasting involves estimating the costs associated with developing, launching, and maintaining your product. This includes both direct costs (e.g., salaries, marketing expenses, cloud infrastructure) and indirect costs (e.g., office rent, utilities, insurance).

Methods for Forecasting Expenses:

- **Budgeting:** Creating a detailed budget that outlines the expected costs for each phase of the product lifecycle.
- **Historical Data Analysis:** Analyzing past expense data to identify trends and patterns that can be used to predict future costs.
- **Vendor Quotes:** Obtaining quotes from vendors for software licenses, hardware, and other expenses.
- **Expert Judgment:** Seeking estimates from experienced team members or subject matter experts.

Best Practices for Forecasting:

- **Start Early:** Begin forecasting as early as possible in the product development process.

- **Involve Key Stakeholders:** Collaborate with finance, marketing, sales, and engineering teams to gather input and ensure accuracy.
- **Use Multiple Methods:** Combine different forecasting methods to improve accuracy and reduce bias.
- **Update Regularly:** Review and update your forecasts regularly based on new information and feedback.
- **Track and Analyze Variances:** Monitor actual performance against your forecasts and analyze any variances to identify potential issues or opportunities.
- **Be Realistic:** Avoid overly optimistic or pessimistic forecasts. Aim for realistic estimates that take into account both potential risks and opportunities.

By mastering the art of forecasting revenue and expenses, product managers can gain greater visibility into the financial future of their products. This enables them to make informed decisions about resource allocation, pricing, marketing, and overall strategy, ultimately ensuring the long-term success and profitability of their products.

13.3 Tracking and Analyzing Financial Performance: Keeping a Pulse on Your Product's Health

Once you've established a budget and revenue projections, the next critical step is to actively track and analyze your product's financial performance. This ongoing process involves monitoring key financial metrics, comparing them to your forecasts, and using the resulting insights to make informed decisions that optimize your product's profitability and sustainability.

Key Financial Metrics for Product Managers:

While financial metrics may seem daunting, understanding a core set is essential for product managers:

1. **Revenue Metrics:**

- **Monthly Recurring Revenue (MRR):** The predictable revenue generated by subscriptions or recurring payments each month.
- **Annual Recurring Revenue (ARR):** The predictable revenue generated annually.
- **Average Revenue Per User (ARPU):** The average revenue generated per user over a specific period.
- **Customer Lifetime Value (LTV):** The total revenue a customer is expected to generate throughout their relationship with your product.
- **Revenue Growth Rate:** The percentage increase in revenue over a specific period.

2. **Cost Metrics:**

- **Customer Acquisition Cost (CAC):** The average cost of acquiring a new customer.
- **Cost of Goods Sold (COGS):** The direct costs associated with producing and delivering your product.
- **Operating Expenses:** The ongoing costs of running your business, such as salaries, marketing, and rent.
- **Gross Margin:** The difference between revenue and COGS, expressed as a percentage of revenue.
- **Net Profit Margin:** The percentage of revenue that remains after all expenses have been paid.

3. **Other Key Metrics:**

- **Burn Rate:** The rate at which a company is spending its capital.
- **Runway:** The amount of time a company can operate before running out of cash.
- **Profit and Loss (P&L) Statement:** A financial statement that summarizes revenues, costs, and expenses over a specific period.
- **Cash Flow Statement:** A financial statement that shows how changes in balance sheet accounts and income affect cash and cash equivalents.

Tools for Tracking and Analyzing Financial Performance:

1. **Financial Modeling Software:** Tools like Excel or Google Sheets can be used to create financial models and forecasts.
2. **Accounting Software:** Software like QuickBooks or Xero can track income and expenses, generate invoices, and prepare financial reports.
3. **Business Intelligence Tools:** Platforms like Tableau or Power BI can visualize financial data and create interactive dashboards.
4. **Subscription Analytics Platforms:** For SaaS businesses, tools like ChartMogul or Baremetrics can track MRR, churn rate, LTV, and other subscription-specific metrics.

Analyzing Financial Performance:

Regularly analyze your financial data to identify trends, understand your financial health, and make informed decisions. Compare your actual performance against your forecasts and investigate any significant variances. Look for patterns and insights that can help you optimize your pricing, marketing, sales, and operational strategies.

Tips for Effective Financial Management:

- **Set Clear Financial Goals:** Define your revenue targets, profitability goals, and other financial objectives.
- **Regularly Review Your Budget and Forecasts:** Don't just set your budget and forget it. Regularly review and update it based on actual performance and market conditions.
- **Monitor Key Metrics:** Track your financial metrics closely and analyze them regularly to identify trends and opportunities for improvement.
- **Control Costs:** Implement cost-saving measures and optimize resource allocation to improve profitability.
- **Seek Professional Guidance:** If you're not familiar with financial management, consider consulting with a financial advisor or accountant to help you develop a sound financial strategy.

By actively tracking and analyzing your financial performance, you can gain valuable insights into your product's profitability, identify areas for improvement, and make data-driven decisions that drive long-term success. Remember, financial management is not just about numbers; it's about understanding the financial health of your product and making strategic decisions that ensure its sustainability and growth.

13.4 Managing Costs and Optimizing Resources: Doing More with Less

In the world of software product management, the efficient allocation and optimization of resources are critical to achieving profitability and long-term success. Product managers must constantly seek ways to reduce costs, maximize the value of their investments, and ensure that resources are aligned with the product strategy and goals. This subchapter will explore various strategies and tactics for managing costs and optimizing resources, empowering you to make the most of your budget and achieve maximum impact with your product.

Cost Management Strategies:

1. Prioritize Ruthlessly:

Not all features or initiatives are created equal. Focus on those that deliver the most value to customers and align with your product strategy. Avoid investing in features that are not essential or that can be postponed to a later stage of development.

2. Optimize Resource Allocation:

Ensure that you have the right resources - people, technology, and budget - allocated to the right tasks at the right time. Avoid overstaffing or understaffing projects, and ensure that your team members have the skills and tools they need to be productive.

3. Negotiate with Vendors:

Don't be afraid to negotiate with vendors for better pricing on software licenses, hardware, cloud services, or other expenses. Consider bundling services or signing longer-term contracts to get discounts.

4. Leverage Open Source Software:

Consider using open-source software where possible to reduce licensing costs. Many high-quality open-source tools and libraries are available for various aspects of product development, such as programming languages, frameworks, and databases.

5. Automate Processes:

Automate repetitive tasks and processes to free up your team's time for more strategic and creative work. This can include using automation tools for testing, deployment, customer support, or marketing.

6. Outsource Non-Core Activities:

Consider outsourcing non-core activities, such as customer support, marketing, or content creation, to external agencies or freelancers. This can help you reduce overhead costs and focus your internal team on core product development activities.

7. Monitor and Control Spending:

Track your expenses closely against your budget to identify any areas where you are overspending or where costs can be reduced. Use expense tracking software or tools to help you monitor and control spending.

8. Track and Analyze Key Metrics:

Monitor key metrics, such as cost per acquisition (CPA), cost per lead (CPL), and return on investment (ROI) for different marketing campaigns and channels. Use this data to optimize your spending and focus on the most effective strategies.

9. Embrace Lean Principles:

Adopt a lean approach to product development, focusing on minimizing waste, maximizing efficiency, and delivering value to customers as quickly as possible. This may involve using agile methodologies, minimizing inventory, and streamlining processes.

10. Review and Adjust Regularly:

Regularly review your budget and spending patterns to identify areas where costs can be reduced or optimized. Don't be afraid to make adjustments to your plans based on new information or changing circumstances.

By implementing these cost management strategies and optimizing your resource allocation, you can maximize the value of your investments, improve your product's profitability, and ensure its long-term success. Remember, effective cost management is not just about cutting costs; it's about making smart decisions that align with your product strategy and deliver the most value to your customers.

13.5 Calculating Return on Investment (ROI): Quantifying Your Product's Success

Return on Investment (ROI) is a crucial financial metric that measures the profitability of your software product relative to the resources invested in it. It is a vital tool for product managers, as it provides a quantitative assessment of the product's financial performance and helps to justify investments in future development and marketing efforts.

Understanding ROI:

ROI is calculated by dividing the net profit (revenue minus expenses) by the total investment cost and expressing the result as a percentage.

ROI = (Net Profit / Total Investment Cost) * 100%

For example, if you invest $100,000 in developing and launching a product and it generates $150,000 in revenue, your net profit is $50,000. Your ROI would then be 50%.

Interpreting ROI:

A positive ROI indicates that the product is generating a return on the investment, while a negative ROI means the product is losing money. The higher the ROI, the more profitable the product is relative to the investment.

It's important to note that ROI is not the only metric to consider when evaluating a product's success. Other factors, such as customer satisfaction, market share, and brand reputation, should also be taken into account. However, ROI is a valuable tool for assessing the financial viability of a product and determining whether it is generating a sufficient return to justify continued investment.

Calculating ROI for Software Products:

Calculating ROI for software products can be challenging, as the investment costs and revenue streams can be complex and vary over time. Here are some tips for calculating ROI for software products:

- **Track All Costs:** Include all costs associated with developing, launching, and maintaining your product, including development costs, marketing and sales expenses, operational costs, and any other relevant expenses.

- **Forecast Revenue Accurately:** Use a combination of methods, such as historical data analysis, market research, and expert judgment, to forecast your product's revenue potential.
- **Consider the Time Value of Money:** The value of money changes over time due to inflation and other factors. Use discounting techniques to adjust future cash flows to their present value.
- **Calculate ROI Over Different Time Periods:** Calculate ROI over different time periods, such as monthly, quarterly, or annually, to get a better understanding of your product's financial performance.
- **Compare ROI to Benchmarks:** Compare your product's ROI to industry benchmarks and similar products to assess its competitiveness.

Using ROI to Inform Product Decisions:

ROI can be a powerful tool for informing product decisions. For example, you can use ROI to:

- **Prioritize Features:** Focus on developing features that are likely to generate the highest ROI.
- **Evaluate Pricing Strategies:** Test different pricing models to see which ones generate the highest ROI.
- **Optimize Marketing Campaigns:** Track the ROI of different marketing campaigns and channels to identify the most effective strategies.
- **Make Investment Decisions:** Use ROI to justify investments in new product development or marketing initiatives.

By calculating and analyzing ROI, product managers can gain valuable insights into the financial performance of their products and make data-driven decisions that drive profitability and growth.

Budgeting and Financial Management Action List

1. Develop a Comprehensive Product Budget:

- Define project scope: Clearly outline the features, functionalities, and deliverables.
- Estimate costs: Gather detailed estimates for personnel, technology, marketing, sales, operations, and contingency expenses.
- Prioritize and allocate resources: Focus on high-value features and allocate resources accordingly.
- Track and monitor expenses: Regularly compare actual spending to the budget.
- Review and adjust: Adapt the budget as the project progresses and new information emerges.

2. Forecast Revenue and Expenses:

- Analyze market size and growth: Research the potential of your target market.
- Determine pricing strategy: Choose a pricing model that aligns with your product and target audience.
- Project customer acquisition and retention: Estimate the number of new and returning customers.
- Assess the competitive landscape: Analyze competitor pricing and offerings.
- Factor in sales and marketing efforts: Consider the impact of your marketing and sales strategies.
- Account for economic conditions: Evaluate the potential impact of economic factors on customer spending.

3. Track and Analyze Financial Performance:

- Monitor revenue metrics: Track MRR, ARR, ARPU, LTV, and revenue growth rate.
- Monitor cost metrics: Track CAC, COGS, operating expenses, gross margin, and net profit margin.
- Analyze financial statements: Review P&L statements and cash flow statements regularly.
- Use financial modeling and accounting software: Leverage tools to track and analyze financial data.
- Compare performance to forecasts: Identify variances and investigate the reasons behind them.

4. Manage Costs and Optimize Resources:

- Prioritize ruthlessly: Focus on high-value features and cut unnecessary expenses.
- Optimize resource allocation: Ensure the right resources are assigned to the right tasks.
- Negotiate with vendors: Seek better pricing and terms for software, hardware, and services.
- Leverage open-source software: Use free and open-source tools where possible.
- Automate processes: Implement automation to reduce manual effort and save time.
- Outsource non-core activities: Consider outsourcing tasks that are not essential to your core competencies.
- Monitor and control spending: Track expenses closely and identify areas for cost reduction.
- Track and analyze key metrics: Use data to optimize marketing and sales spending.
- Embrace lean principles: Minimize waste and maximize efficiency in your processes.

- Review and adjust regularly: Adapt your budget and spending based on new information and changing circumstances.

5. Calculate Return on Investment (ROI):

- Track all costs: Include development, marketing, sales, operations, and other relevant expenses.
- Forecast revenue accurately: Use multiple methods to estimate your product's revenue potential.
- Consider the time value of money: Discount future cash flows to their present value.
- Calculate ROI over different time periods: Analyze monthly, quarterly, and annual ROI.
- Compare ROI to benchmarks: Assess your product's performance against industry standards.
- Use ROI to inform decisions: Prioritize features, evaluate pricing, and optimize marketing based on ROI.

By taking these actions, you can establish a solid foundation for financial management in your product development process, ensuring your product is not only innovative and user-friendly but also financially viable and profitable in the long run.

Conclusion: The Path to Product Excellence

Throughout this book, we've embarked on a comprehensive journey through the multifaceted world of software product management. We've explored the foundational principles, strategic frameworks, tactical approaches, and emerging trends that shape the role of the product manager in the ever-evolving technology landscape.

Key Principles and Takeaways:

- **The Product Manager as the Central Orchestrator:** Product managers are the linchpin of the product development process, bridging the gap between business, technology, and user needs. They are the visionaries, strategists, and leaders who guide the product from conception to launch and beyond.
- **The Importance of Vision and Strategy:** A clear and compelling vision serves as the guiding star for the product team, while a well-defined strategy provides the roadmap to achieving that vision. Together, they create a sense of purpose, alignment, and direction for the entire organization.
- **Customer-Centricity at the Core:** Understanding your customers' needs, preferences, and behaviors is fundamental to building successful products. User research, feedback collection, and data analysis are essential tools for gaining insights into the customer's world and tailoring your product accordingly.
- **Data-Driven Decision Making:** In the digital age, data is the lifeblood of product management.

Leverage data analytics and experimentation to validate assumptions, measure progress, identify opportunities, and make informed decisions that drive product success.

- **Agile Development and Iteration:** Embrace agile methodologies to foster flexibility, collaboration, and continuous improvement. Iterate on your product based on user feedback and data to ensure it remains relevant and competitive.
- **Effective Communication and Collaboration:** Building strong relationships and fostering open communication with stakeholders, team members, and customers is crucial for successful product management.
- **Financial Acumen:** Understand the financial aspects of product development, from budgeting and forecasting to measuring ROI, to ensure your product is not only innovative but also financially viable.
- **Ethical Considerations:** As software products become more pervasive and impactful, product managers must grapple with ethical considerations such as data privacy, bias, transparency, and accessibility. Building responsible products is not only a moral imperative but also a strategic advantage.
- **Embracing Emerging Trends:** Stay abreast of emerging trends such as AI, machine learning, and data-driven product management to leverage these technologies to enhance your product development process and deliver more personalized and engaging user experiences.

By internalizing these key principles and applying the strategies and tactics outlined in this book, you can elevate your product management practice, navigate the complexities of the software industry, and create products that truly make a difference in the world.

The Future of Software Product Management: Embracing Change and Driving Innovation

The landscape of software product management is in a constant state of evolution, shaped by technological advancements, shifting market dynamics, and evolving customer expectations. As we look ahead, several key trends are poised to redefine the role of the product manager and reshape the future of product development and delivery.

1. The Rise of AI and ML:

Artificial Intelligence and Machine Learning will play an increasingly prominent role in product management. AI-powered tools will automate routine tasks, analyze vast amounts of data, and generate actionable insights, freeing up product managers to focus on strategic decision-making and innovation. ML algorithms will enable personalized user experiences, predictive analytics, and intelligent automation, transforming how products are designed, developed, and marketed.

2. Data-Driven Decision Making:

Data will become even more central to product management. Product managers will rely on data analytics, A/B testing, and experimentation to validate assumptions, measure impact, and optimize product performance. This data-driven approach will lead to more informed decisions, faster iterations, and ultimately, more successful products.

3. Customer-Centricity at Scale:

With the proliferation of digital channels and touchpoints, understanding and meeting customer needs will be more crucial than ever. Product managers will leverage advanced analytics, user feedback tools, and machine learning to gain deep insights into customer behavior and preferences. This will enable them to create highly personalized experiences that resonate with individual users, driving engagement, loyalty, and advocacy.

4. Agile and DevOps Integration:

The integration of Agile development methodologies and DevOps practices will become the norm. Product managers will work closely with cross-functional teams, embracing a culture of collaboration, continuous delivery, and rapid iteration. This will enable them to respond quickly to market changes, release new features and updates more frequently, and deliver value to customers at an accelerated pace.

5. Ethical Product Management:

As software products become more pervasive and impactful, ethical considerations will take center stage. Product managers will need to grapple with issues such as data privacy, algorithm bias, transparency, and the societal impact of their products. Ethical product management will become a core competency, ensuring that products are not only innovative and profitable but also responsible and beneficial to society.

6. The Rise of the Product-Led Growth (PLG) Model:

PLG is a go-to-market strategy that relies on the product itself as the primary driver of customer acquisition, conversion, and expansion. This approach emphasizes delivering exceptional user experiences, leveraging product usage data for insights, and optimizing the product to drive organic growth. Product managers will need to master the principles of PLG to build products that are not only valuable but also inherently engaging and easy to adopt.

7. Continuous Learning and Upskilling:

The rapid pace of technological change will require product managers to continuously update their skills and knowledge. They will need to stay abreast of emerging trends, master new tools and technologies, and develop a deep understanding of AI, ML, and data analytics. Continuous learning and upskilling will be essential for staying relevant and competitive in this ever-evolving field.

Conclusion:

The future of software product management is brimming with exciting possibilities. By embracing technological advancements, prioritizing customer-centricity, adopting data-driven practices, and upholding ethical principles, product managers can shape the future of software and create products that not only meet market demands but also enrich the lives of users and make a positive impact on the world.

Resources for Continued Learning: Fueling Your Product Management Journey

The field of software product management is constantly evolving, demanding continuous learning and adaptation from its practitioners. To stay ahead of the curve and excel in your role, it's essential to tap into a variety of resources that can expand your knowledge, hone your skills, and provide inspiration. Here's a comprehensive list of resources to fuel your continued learning:

Books: Please note that these link to my Amazon Affiliate site.

- Inspired: How to Create Tech Products Customers Love by Marty Cagan
- The Lean Product Playbook by Dan Olsen
- Empowered: Ordinary People, Extraordinary Products by Marty Cagan and Chris Jones
- The Product Manager Interview by Lewis C. Lin
- Continuous Discovery Habits by Teresa Torres
- Escaping the Build Trap by Melissa Perri
- Hooked: How to Build Habit-Forming Products by Nir Eyal
- Crossing the Chasm by Geoffrey A. Moore

Online Courses and Certifications:

- **Product Management 101** by Udemy
- **Product Management First Steps** by LinkedIn Learning
- **Product Management Fundamentals Professional Certificate** by Coursera

- The Association of International Product Marketing and Management (AIPMM) certifications
- Pragmatic Institute Product Management courses
- Reforge programs

Blogs and Websites:

- Silicon Valley Product Group (SVPG)
- Mind the Product
- The Product Coalition
- Product School
- Roman Pichler's Blog
- Ken Norton's Blog
- Bringing the Donuts

Podcasts:

- This is Product Management
- The Product Podcast
- Masters of Scale
- The Product Experience
- Product Hunt Radio

Conferences and Events:

- Mind the Product Conference
- Industry: The Product Conference
- ProductCon
- Women in Product Conference

Online Communities:

- Mind the Product Slack Community
- Product School Pro Community

- **Product Manager HQ**
- **Women in Product (various chapters)**
- **The Product Folks**

Newsletters:

- **Product Mindset**
- **The Product Manager's Newsletter**
- **Inside Intercom**
- **Lenny's Newsletter**

Mentorship and Networking:

- **Seek out mentors** in your network or through online platforms like ADPList.
- **Join professional organizations** like the Product Management Association (PMA) or Women in Product.
- **Attend networking events** and meetups to connect with other product managers and learn from their experiences.

Continuous Learning Tips:

- **Set learning goals:** Define what you want to learn and set specific, measurable goals to track your progress.
- **Make time for learning:** Schedule dedicated time each week for learning and development.
- **Experiment and apply:** Don't just consume information; apply what you learn to your work and experiment with new approaches.
- **Share your knowledge:** Teach others what you have learned through blog posts, presentations, or mentoring.

- **Stay curious:** Never stop asking questions, exploring new ideas, and seeking out new knowledge.

By actively engaging with these resources and making a commitment to continuous learning, you can stay at the forefront of the product management field, develop your skills, expand your network, and ultimately achieve greater success in your career.

Recap and Final Thoughts: Embarking on Your Product Management Journey

As we reach the end of this comprehensive guide to software product management, let's take a moment to reflect on the key takeaways and insights that have emerged from our exploration.

Throughout this book, we have traversed the entire product lifecycle, from ideation and discovery to launch and optimization. We have delved into the core principles, strategies, and tactics that empower product managers to create innovative, user-friendly, and commercially successful software products. We have explored the importance of defining a clear vision and strategy, conducting thorough market research, prioritizing features, managing cross-functional teams, crafting compelling marketing campaigns, and making data-driven decisions.

We have also examined the emerging trends that are shaping the future of product management, such as the growing influence of AI and ML, the rise of data-driven decision-making, the importance of customer-centricity, and the ethical considerations that must be addressed in the development and deployment of software products.

The path of a product manager is not always smooth. It is fraught with challenges, setbacks, and difficult decisions. However, by understanding the common mistakes to avoid, learning from the experiences of others, and equipping yourself with the right tools and knowledge, you can navigate this complex landscape with confidence and achieve lasting success.

Remember, product management is not just a job; it's a calling. It is a profession that demands passion, dedication, creativity, and a relentless focus on delivering value to users. As technology continues to evolve at an unprecedented pace, the role of the product manager will only become more critical. It is up to you to embrace the challenges, seize the opportunities, and shape the future of software.

Final Thoughts:

The journey of a product manager is a continuous learning process. It requires a thirst for knowledge, a willingness to experiment, and an unwavering commitment to improvement. The resources and insights shared in this book are just the beginning. I encourage you to continue learning, exploring, and pushing the boundaries of what's possible in the world of software product management.

Stay curious, stay adaptable, and never stop learning. The future of software is yours to shape.

Sources

- The Trendy Coder: Agile Cheat Sheet for Beginners: https://thetrendycoder.com/agile-cheat-sheet-for-beginners/
- Animo-GD's Data Analysis Roadmap: https://github.com/Animo-GD/Data-Analysis-RoadMap
- Tulio Calil's JavaScript for Data Analytics: https://tuliocalil.com/javascript-for-data-analytics/
- Wikipedia: Scrum (Software Development): https://en.wikipedia.org/wiki/Scrum_(software_development)
- HighRadius Blog: Don't Understand Cloud Computing? You're Not Alone: https://www.highradius.com/resources/Blog/dont-understand-cloud-computing-youre-not-alone/
- Wikipedia: On-Premises Software: https://en.wikipedia.org/wiki/On-premises_software
- Voice of Shark on Medium: How to Become a Successful Entrepreneur in 2023: https://medium.com/@voiceofshark/how-to-become-a-successful-entrepreneur-in-2023-e8157c5a9bf3
- Vorombe Tech on Medium: Navigating the Evolving Landscape of Data Privacy Regulations: [invalid URL removed]
- Jolly Good Photo: Data Protection and GDPR Compliance Policy: https://www.jollygoodphoto.co.uk/data-protection-and-gdpr-compliance-policy.html
- Secure Privacy AI Blog: Cookie Consent Management Platforms: https://secureprivacy.ai/blog/cookie-consent-management-platforms
- GovDocs: Disclosing Bipolar Disorder: Key Discrimination Claims: https://www.govdocs.com/disclosing-bipolar-disorder-key-discrimination-claims/

- City of Bloomington: News on Disability Discrimination: https://bloomington.in.gov/news/2022/07/12/5230
- Deque University: Accessibility Glossary: https://docs.deque.com/devtools-html/4.0.0/en/glossary

- GetAccept Blog: Nurturing Collaboration: https://www.getaccept.com/blog/nurture-collaboration

www.ingramcontent.com/pod-product-compliance
Lightning Source LLC
LaVergne TN
LVHW051320050326
832903LV00031B/3270